My Reflections *on* Nepal's Constitution, Governance *and* Politics

गणेश राज शर्मा

My Reflections *on* Nepal's Constitution, Governance *and* Politics

Ganesh Raj Sharma

MANDALA BOOK POINT
"BOOKS FOR ENLIGHTENMENT"
Kantipath, G.P.O. Box 528, Kathmandu

First edition published in 2022 by
Mandala Book Point
Kantipath, G.P.O. Box: 528, Kathmandu, Nepal
Tel: 977-1-4249555, 4227711, 4255444, Fax: 977-1-4255921
e-mail: books@mos.com.np

ISBN 978-99933-42-57-1

Printed and bound by
Dongol Printers, Kathmandu
Tel.: 977-1-4281682
e-mail: dongolprinters@gmail.com

To Niru
who made it all possible

Contents

Foreword

I am delighted to write the foreword to this collection of essays and interviews entitled "My Reflections on Nepal's Constitution, Governance and Politics" by the late Ganesh Raj Sharma.

I first met Ganeshji about fifty years ago. He was a lawyer of extraordinary caliber, vision, and integrity.

When Nepal embraced democracy in 1950, there was a crying need for establishing an independent judiciary, rule of law, and constitutionalism, and for defining people's rights under the constitution. Doing so required modernizing the country's legal and judicial system. A handful of talented judges and lawyers took up this challenge. Ganeshji was one of them. They commenced the work of transforming the praxis and culture of the judicial system in Nepal and that transformation became the country's foundation of a system of constitutional recourse, remedy, and writ jurisprudence. These talented young men led by example and helped orient the next generation of colleagues.

Ganeshji's unflinching faith in the rule of law in a democracy was exemplary. He came to the limelight through court cases in which he defended many political prisoners who had suffered at the hands of an authoritarian government that was established in 1960 by the then King by dismissing Nepal's first democratically elected parliament and the prime minister. Amongst the political prisoners he defended was the late B.P. Koirala.

Ganeshji played an active role in the Bar Association in the 1970s.

The promulgation of the 1990 Constitution established a constitutional monarchy, multiparty democracy, and an independent judiciary. Ganeshji played a pivotal role in many landmark constitutional cases during his career. These included the dissolution of the parliament (four times during his career); a water-sharing treaty with India; the citizenship Bill; employment of foreign labourers and many others. He was an early champion of public-interest jurisprudence. His arguments were based on rigourous research and were of high intellectual caliber. His presentations were clear, powerful, and convincing. He was a highly sought after amicus.

This collection of essays and interviews portrays the essence of Ganeshji, as one of Nepal's foremost independent thinkers, a patriot who fought for sustainable peace, democracy, and the prosperity of the nation. The core issues he advocated were permanent transit rights, non-reciprocity in bilateral ties, especially with India, and fair trade deals and fair treatment in economic matters.

He was bold and did not hesitate to advance unpopular views if he was convinced they were good for Nepal. Concerning the labour disputes with India, he said:

"With a population of 20 million, Nepal cannot be expected to offer job opportunities to 1 billion population in India. Reciprocity in such a matter would eliminate Nepal's identity and Nepalis would find themselves as a minority in their own nation. Migration of Nepal's entire population would be an insignificant minority."

Ganeshji strongly held the view that both India and China should treat Nepal based on sovereign equality, justice, and fairness, regardless of the difference in the sizes of our respective countries. He argued that the recognition of the special constraints of small nations, such as their lack of negotiating capacity, is a sine qua non for the development of healthy regional and international relations. He took the view that since international relations are guided by national interest, rather than by principles, special care needs to be taken in protecting the interest and concerns of small countries like Nepal.

His writings also reflect his long-held and consistent views on matters such as economic development, representative democracy, electoral reforms, corruption control, and constitutional reforms. Although these essays reflect events of the past, given the evolving nature of the constitution, as well as the economic and political turbulence that is still present in the country, they are, in my mind, still relevant. At the very least, they provide a historical perspective to the understanding of present problems.

Readers may not agree with some of Ganeshji's views. A committed democrat, he recognized and appreciated that democracy is a market of thoughts, opinions, arguments, and beliefs. Ganeshji would have appreciated any contrary views.

Ganeshji is highly respected for the academic rigour in his works and his professional integrity. He expressed his views sincerely and candidly. I recommend this book to any reader who has an interest in Nepali law, justice, and politics.

I would also like to congratulate the publisher, Madhab Maharjan of Mandala for bringing "My Reflections on Nepal's Constitution, Governance and Politics" to readers in Nepal and abroad.

KALYAN SHRESTHA
Former Chief Justice of Nepal

December 2021 (Yomari Punhi)
२०७८ पौष ४ गते, योमरी पुन्ही

Publisher's Note

My first personal acquaintance with late Ganesh Raj Sharma was after the restoration of multi-party democracy in Nepal in 1990. At that time, ours was a relation between a book trader and a book love, who was already a well-known social figure with a wide scholarly interest. He would often visit Mandala Book Point to browse and buy books for his personal study. He would occasionally suggest us to add to our collection scholarly books by prominent authors and publishers on a wide range of subjects including politics, current affairs, constitutional law, social sciences, and literature. Ganesh Raj-ji was always complimentary about Mandala Book Point's engagement in publishing scholarly books and research works in Nepal even in those early days.

I am delighted by the fact that quite a number of reputed academics, scholars and others, both from Nepal and abroad, have found our bookstore very useful and continue to inspire and support us in this endeavour. This is one of the most important reasons that motivate us to continue in this business, even during difficult times such as the ones we are going through at the moment. Had profit been our only motive, we would have chosen to opt for some other vocation. However, we in the Mandala Book Point are driven by a deeply held belief that free flow of knowledge and information through the medium of books remains one of the most effective means to develop a nation's reserve of creative and productive assets.

I have already spent more than half a century of my life in book trade, and have come a long way, through numerous vicissitudes, beginning with the hippie days in the early 1970s, to the Panchayat era, the multi-party democracy, and more recently to the Federal Democratic Republic of Nepal. Since the 1990s, book traders have had to face periodic attempts by the government to impose customs duty and taxes (three times in three decades from 1990 to 2020) on the import of books, from India as well as other countries. For a country still struggling to attain universal literacy level and also trying to broaden and upgrade the quality of higher education in keeping with the demands of a rapidly globalizing world, we worry that such prohibitive impositions would only discourage the readers and disincentives the fledgling business of book trade. Each time this happens, a state of utter confusion, uncertainty, and disbelief permeates into this sector. Although two such earlier attempts of the government had to be quickly revoked because of public outcry and opposition, the latest one in 2019 lingered on for more than a year and a half, despite sustained opposition and protest from a wider section of the conscience keepers of society – scholars, academicians, students, legal practitioners, opinion writers, media personalities and media houses. With the onset of Covid-19 pandemic, book traders already facing the unpleasant prospect of closing down their businesses due to the adverse government policy have had confront yet another new challenge to their business. It was at this crucial point of time that the new finance minister took the decision on 10 November 2020 to do away with the customs duty that had been imposed on book imports. We in the book trade business gratefully welcomed this long-awaited decision. I should also add at this point that Ganesh Raj-ji was one of those individuals who strongly advocated against tax and duty imposition on book imports, and always spoke in support of the book traders' movements to that effect.

Regarding this book and its author, senior advocate and learned legal scholar Ganesh Raj Sharma, his demise in 2015 was indeed a great loss to the nation. In his almost five decades of active legal service, he stood firm on principles and values that he upheld as true and indispensable. He never shrank from defending them to the hilt. He was a superb constitutional lawyer, a well-informed legal scholar, a public intellectual and a political analyst with prescience and acuity. Although he was not always appreciated by his colleagues or contemporaries, he remained largely respected for his unwavering integrity and professionalism. As a constitutional lawyer, he believed in the principles of constitutional supremacy and the rule of law. He provided professional legal services to all seeking justice, including politicians, irrespective of class or political affiliation. He was able to leave his indelible mark in respect of landmark cases that significantly impacted the nation's judicial and constitutional system. Whenever the nation was at a crossroads of crucial constitutional dilemmas, Ganesh Raj Sharma's interpretation of the letter and spirit of the constitution and the law remained timely and relevant as did his vision of foundational democratic values and principles and the rule of law.

Sometime after his demise, I received a call from Mridu Sharma Chand, Ganesh Raj-ji's daughter regarding publication of a collection of her late father's manuscripts. I visited her at Ganesh Raj-ji's residence in Dhobidhara, accompanied by Ganesh Dutta Bhatta, associate professor at Nepal Law Campus. She shared with me a collection of Ganesh Raj-ji's articles systematically arranged in a folder – by the author himself with the unspoken intent of publishing it in a book form. In view of my good relationship with the author and as Mriduji also wished to see her father's work published, I happily agreed to cooperate with her in this regard.

The onerous task of editing took some time. My colleague Ganesh Khaniya, who by profession is an engineer but also holds an M. Phil. degree in English literature, along with Ms. Nabina Basukala, a student of English literature, initially helped sort out typographical errors and uniformity in style. Meanwhile, due to the COVID-19 pandemic and the resultant lockdowns and other health-related regulatory measures, our work was interrupted and got delayed. Through Mriduji, we also contacted Jan Sharma, a writer, who graciously went through the manuscript several times, and provided important insights as someone quite close to Ganesh Raj ji and his thoughts and writings. In the beginning of 2021, I also sought the assistance of a friend of mine (who prefers anonymity) who extended substantial help in verifying citations made in the book that required re-searching the original sources.

On behalf of Mandala Book Point, I am delighted to bring out this book in the present form. It was in close consultation with the author's family that we decided to give it the title: **My Reflections on Nepal's Constitution, Governance and Politics** by ***Ganesh Raj Sharma***. I humbly take the responsibility for any editorial lapses that might have escaped the editorial eyes. We hope to correct them in the next edition.

Last, but not the least, I am grateful to Mriduji and her family for entrusting me with the publication of this important book. I am deeply indebted to the esteemed former Chief Justice Mr. Kalyan Shrestha for readily accepting my request to write a foreword to this book.

MADHAB LAL MAHARJAN
Kathmandu

December 2021

Acknowledgements

My father, Ganesh Raj Sharma, passed away on October 27, 2015. During his life, he was known for his independent opinions and in-depth analyses of current political and legal affairs. This book is an anthology of his thoughts and analyses that have previously appeared in print or in presentations.

My father shared with me that he had compiled his writings, saying he was not yet sure what he wanted to do with these. While clearing his office after his passing, I came upon two folders of neatly typed articles, stapled, and arranged in order, and titled, in his handwriting, "*mera samayik abhibyaktiharu* (मेरा सामयिक अभिव्यक्तिहरू) etc.". Most of these articles were printed on a traditional typewriter, some through a more modern word processor by Mr. Birat Govind Shrestha, whose dedication to my father I acknowledge.

One day, during my stay in Kathmandu after his demise, I found myself at the Mandala Book Point, a bookstore I knew he had frequented during his life. When I found that Mandala was in the publishing business as well, I reached out to Mr. Madhab Maharjan, the Chief of Mandala and an old acquaintance of my father's to ask if he would be interested in publishing an anthology of my father's writings. He expressed a keen interest in the project. This book is a result of that conversation. I am immensely grateful to Mr. Maharjan for his time, commitment, enthusiasm, and support in bringing this anthology together.

I do not share my father's particular intellectual background in Nepalese politics and law. As I was going through this anthology, I keenly missed him, wishing he was around to expound on the context and content. I was, however, able to engage Mr. Jan Sharma, my cousin, to whom I am immensely grateful for patiently going through the manuscript multiple times, providing context and clarification when needed. My sincere gratitude also to Naresh Koirala, my maternal uncle, for going through the manuscript as well as providing critical and constructive feedback. The two of them, along with my immediate family, Mohan, my husband, and my children, Ro and Syon, helped me with the selection of title of the book.

This book is dedicated in its entirety to my mother, Nirmala Sharma, without whom, in my father's own words, he would not have attained and exercised the vast intellectual freedom he treasured.

Mridu Sharma Chand
Asheville, NC

October 27, 2021

I

Nepal's Experiment in Representation

Governance through popular representation evolved gradually in Nepal before universal adult franchise was constitutionally adopted. Historically, Nepal has a record of uninterrupted independence, with its own traditions traceable even in ancient Hindu and Buddhist scriptures. As a multi-ethnic, multi-religious and multi-lingual nation, Nepal has social and cultural roots for a moderate and pluralistic society. Assimilating and reconciling influences between two ancient civilisations of Asia, Nepal all along lived with its indigenous polity. With a minimum involvement of the state, villages were primary units of self-governing institution, traditionally known as the panchayat. Even the institution of monarchy commanded allegiance based on popular, rather than divine, power to rule. Consensus, not conquest, was a prominent attribute of monarchy in Nepal. Revered King Drabya Shah was made the king in Liglig in Gorkha, where Gurungs had a tradition of electing their leader, a tradition which had an impact on the functioning of the Shah kings. Persuasion and consent were the basis on which the ancestors of the Shah kings built up a reputation for justice in Gorkha. A body of councils represented popular will in governance.

Following that tradition, King Prithvi Narayan Shah, who had the honour of unifying modern Nepal, expressed his vision for the nation in his famous sermon in these words: "I observed the arrangements of King Ram Shah, I saw the arrangements of Jayasthiti Malla also. …Let the king not kill a servant in his house. Let the king see that justice is done. Let there be no injustice in our country." He expressed his personal view that he wanted to make Biraj Bakheti his prime minister, but he named Kalu Pande to the job because this was the popular will. Despite reversals in practice, theoretically there was a trend towards the supremacy of the popular will in governance. This was at a time when major industrial democracies were in a drive to colonise countries across continents. Close to Nepal, the French were fighting a losing battle against the British in India. Americans were fighting for their independence and the French were preparing for their historic revolution. Nepal, isolated from the rest of the world, was in the process of unifying the nation in 1769.

The tradition of rule through councils and popular will came to an end after prolonged court conspiracies and the Kot Massacre of 1846. A family oligarchy prevailed over the king. A system of hereditary prime minister with absolute power continued until the Rana oligarchy was overthrown in 1951 by a popular uprising with the backing of the king. Meanwhile, momentous changes took place in both of Nepal's neighbours following the termination of World War II. India's independence and the liberation of China caused a political sensation in Nepal as well. The liberal-minded Prime Minister

Padma Shumsher tried to introduce reforms under the hereditary prime ministerial rule and India's Prime Minister Jawaharlal Nehru provided constitutional expertise to draft a constitution. But the Constitution of 1948 failed before it was ever put into practice because of its inherent contradictions. A grand compromise ended the attempted revolution with the commitment to elect a constituent assembly to draft a constitution. Before the election was held, the Interim Government of Nepal Act of 1951 was introduced. It abrogated the Constitution of 1948.

Originally, this act was intended to draft a democratic constitution within two years, but that process was prolonged until 1958 due to a crisis of readjustment between traditional and modernizing forces. During the interim period, several advisory assemblies were constituted by nomination, and several forms of governments by nominated persons were experimented with. This was a period of rehearsals and apprenticeship for a parliamentary democracy and a cabinet system of government. Ultimately, instead of the promised constituent assembly, the king garnered popular consensus for a constitution which he finalised in 1958.

Representatives of prominent political parties and British constitutional expert Sir Ivor Jennings were included in the drafting committee. Unfortunately, like all other constitutions of Third World countries drafted by Jennings, the Constitution of the Kingdom of Nepal 1959 was rejected by the body polity of Nepal. The two houses of parliament and the king were, in essence, sovereign. Though the king had ample discretion to overrule the government and the legislature, abuse of that discretion was sure to be counterproductive. Very wisely, a system of checks and balances was inserted in the constitution based on the practical experience of the constitutional monarchy in Britain. Once the parameters of the constitution were violated in spirit, it would not survive in letter either.

While submitting the draft of the constitution, Sir Ivor Jennings made the following points in his explanatory memorandum:

> The commission prepared a draft similar in its principles to the constitutions of other countries in Asia operating under a parliamentary system of government but with modifications which distinguish a constitutional monarchy from a federal state. The general scheme was as follows:
>
> 1) Executive authority was vested in His Majesty, but general direction and control of administration were vested in a cabinet responsible to Parliament. Because the parliamentary system was new to Nepal, and accordingly, guidance could not be sought from constitutional convention, care was taken to define, with such precision as the changing circumstances of government allowed, the relation between His Majesty and his ministers.
>
> 2) Parliament was to consist of two houses, called, in the English text, the House of Representatives and the Senate. The House of Representatives was to consist wholly of members elected by the electors voting in single-member constituencies by secret ballot, and adult franchise was provided. There was to be a general election every five years, or more often if His Majesty dissolved Parliament on the recommendation of the cabinet. The Senate was to consist of persons appointed by His Majesty on the recommendation of the prime minister. When Parliament is dissolved, the senators will retain their seats, but one-third of the senators will retire every two years. Provision was made for the House of Representatives, as the elected House, to override the Senate, except with respect to

constitutional amendments, and the cabinet was to be collectively responsible to the House of Representatives. All legislation was to require royal assent, however in certain circumstances, His Majesty could withhold assent.

What Western democracies, particularly Britain, had achieved in a post-industrial evolution was being implemented in a traditional society which lacked not only a pre-industrial situation but also an organised mercantile system. A constitution made for parliamentary supremacy, therefore, produced a village-based guided democracy. In his justification of his action, King Mahendra denounced the Western model of democracy as unsuitable to the genius of the Nepali people. He did hope to revert to full-fledged parliamentary democracy at the base, but the switch was delayed during three decades of uneasiness. Nepal was not alone in this phase of political experiment. That was a period when most developing countries, after gaining independence from colonial rule, succumbed to various forms of unpopular and non-representative governments. Indonesia, under the leadership of Sukarno, experimented with a guided democracy to fulfill Sukarno's dream of ameliorating the miseries of the masses faster than in a normal democratic way. Nasser of Egypt had the same illusion about guided democracy. In Pakistan, Ayub Khan was trying "basic democracy" to develop a grassroots democracy with a limited franchise. The cold-war situation in the world made the process of democracy very unstable. Nepal faced the additional threat of political polarisation being converted into a proxy war between big neighbouring countries. Political parties were considered vulnerable to political polarisation linked with the forces of the cold war. Western democracies were more concerned for their global security than for supporting fledgling democracies in the Third World. Thus, there were no tears shed by the democratic world when democracy was rejected in Nepal.

When Nepal started with parliamentary democracy in 1959, disenchantment had already set in other democracies. Persons like Jayaprakash Narayan in India said, "I personally and fully believe that it is possible to develop a party-less democracy." Disappointed by the socialist movement which he had led so vigorously, he was creating hope for an alternative to "the framework of Western democracy." He uttered scathing criticism against the functioning of political parties in India:

> "The party system, with the corroding and corrupting struggles for power inherent in it, disturbed me more and more. I saw how parties backed by finance, organisation and the means of propaganda could impose themselves on the people; how people's rule became, in effect, party rule; how party rule, in turn, became the rule of caucus and coterie; how democracy was reduced to mere casting of votes; how even this right to vote was restricted severely by the system of powerful parties setting up their candidates from who alone, for all practical purposes, the voters had to make their choice; how even this limited choice was made unreal by the fact that the issues posed before the electorate were, by and large, incomprehensible to it.
>
> The party system as I saw it was emasculating the people. It did not function so as to develop their strength and initiative, nor to help them establish their self-rule and to manage their affairs themselves. All that the parties were concerned with was to rule over the people, no doubt, with their consent. The party system, so it appeared to me, was seeking to reduce the people to the position of sheep whose only function of sovereignty would be to choose periodically

> the shepherd who would look after their affairs. This, to me, did not spell freedom—the freedom, the Swaraj, for which I had fought and for which the people of this country had fought."

All these debates perhaps inspired and encouraged King Mahendra to stand against a multiparty system. As Crown Prince, he had already expressed his annoyance by criticising political parties for not behaving according to the norms of democracy. He found himself very close to those who were in search of an alternative model of democracy suitable for a developing country. It was disclosed by a former prime minister, Dr. Tulsi Giri, that a draft of the constitution that had panchayats and an indirect method of election to the National Panchayat had been forwarded to Jayaprakash Narayan for consideration. His reactions are unknown. But in support of that constitutional arrangement, a Gandhian scholar, Shriman Narayan Agarwal, who was also India's ambassador to Nepal, had said in his recollection: "In a small and developing country like Nepal, I personally see no harm in this type of democratic system. Even Gandhiji pleaded for direct democracy at the base and indirect elections upwards."

The Constitution of 1962 formalised the panchayat as a system of governance on a tiered basis in the first phase. Exercising his inherent prerogative, the king promulgated a new constitution in 1962. Emphasising the growth of a grassroots representative system in the form of a guided democracy, the constitution advocated the supremacy of the parliament, which had no favourable situation in which to survive. Though political parties were banned, the constitution remained silent about partylessness, which became a feature of the constitution by the First Amendment to the constitution on 28 January 1967, expanding the base of the electorate and keeping the tier system intact. The growing involvement of the people in the political process increased political polarisation, a state which rendered partylessness practically irrelevant. The Second Amendment of the constitution, adopted in 1975, again broadened the electorate but introduced a party-like body known as the Go-to-the-Village National Campaign (Gaun Farka Rashtriya Aviyan) to curb and harmonise conflicts of political interests and ideas.

The pressure being built up from both within and outside the panchayat was so acute that the panchayat system was put to test in a national referendum in 1980. The referendum offered two options: the panchayat system with gradual reforms or a multiparty system. The result was in favour of gradual reforms in the political system. The Third Amendment was introduced in 1980. It made three major reforms. First, the Rashtriya Panchayat, the national assembly, was to be constituted mainly on the basis of direct adult franchise. Second, the prime minister was to be elected by a majority vote by the members of the legislature. Third, the council of ministers was responsible to the house, individually as well as collectively.

However, a stipulation requiring members of the Rashtriya Panchayat to be members of any of the class organisations under the guidance and control of a political body of the panchayat was a stymie to the pluralist political activities in process. Even for the most conciliatory of politicians, such as B.P. Koirala, participation in the election was not acceptable. The motive behind the reform was to preserve the panchayat system, whereas almost all political parties wanted an alternative pluralist political system. The amendment was not enough to satisfy political parties. So, in 1989-90 the panchayat system again passed through political confrontation and an upheaval of very serious dimensions. Realising the alarming situation in the country, an all-party consensus was reached at King Birendra's initiative. It was an extraordinary consensus reached in an extraordinary situation which decided a model of change for the future. The Constitution of the Kingdom of Nepal 1990 was the outcome of that extraordinary consensus.

Though authoritarian in structure, there had been a great constitutional exercise within the panchayat system had forced gradual reforms. A large number of Supreme Court cases can be cited as reflecting the nature of the constitutional struggle for the rights of the people as well as institutional developments. In the apex national legislature, attempts were made for political performance of the nature of a parliamentary democracy and the accountability of the government. But the most significant development of democracy was at the lowest unit of the panchayat system in the form of local self-government. About four thousand villages and thirty-six towns were incorporated as units of local self-government. Apprenticeship in governance was developed through these local bodies, which can be a matter of separate discussion. In essence, this development made the masses politically educated despite rampant illiteracy. A situation for a comprehensive change in the political system to accommodate all segments of people was maturing. A lesson was imparted by the experience: direct adult franchise and a partyless system were incompatible. As the reforms could not meet the popular demand, they could not accommodate the political parties. In 1990 the country faced a great upheaval which ended in a compromise for multiparty democracy with constitutional monarchy. The Constitution of the Kingdom of Nepal 1990 was the outcome. This was the country's fifth written constitution in five decades in its quest for an appropriate form of a representative governance.

The 1990 Constitution was drafted keeping past experiences in mind. Though multiparty democracy was revived, the Constitution of 1959, which provided for a multiparty system, was not. The previous constitution was not considered as having had adequate checks on the arbitrary use of discretionary powers, particularly by the head of the state. Many restrictions were imposed upon the executive powers of the state. In a way, it could be termed a rigid constitution. That rigidity was almost deliberate because of the negative experience of the past. The most prominent part in the Constitution is the declaration of its basic features. According to Article 116, the Constitution cannot be amended contravening the spirit of its Preamble, which calls for the nature of the governance to be as follows:

> "And whereas, it is expedient to promulgate and enforce this Constitution, made with the widest possible participation of the Nepalese people, to guarantee basic human rights to every citizen of Nepal; and also to consolidate the adult franchise, the parliamentary system of government, constitutional monarchy and the system of multiparty democracy by promoting amongst the people of Nepal the spirit of fraternity and the bond of unity on the basis of liberty and equality; and also to establish an independent and competent system of justice with a view to transforming the concept of the rule of law into a living reality."

> Article 24 (4) includes a provision on representation: "It shall be the chief responsibility of the state to maintain conditions suitable to enjoyment of the fruits of democracy

through wider participation of the people in governance of the country and by way of decentralisation, and to promote general welfare by making provisions for the protection and promotion of human rights, by maintaining tranquillity and order in the society."

Though there is an expression regarding "wider participation of the people in the governance by way of decentralisation," the Constitution intended to let parliament determine the quantum of such decentralisation. The whole edifice of local self-government would have come to a standstill had there been no compulsion to constitute it for the purpose of electing one-fourth of the members of the Upper House from the local units of self-government.

The prime minister had specific instruction to leave the local self-government units completely on parliamentary legislation. Despite an indirect but mandatory provision in the constitution to constitute local government units as an electorate for one-fourth of the members of the upper house of parliament, the prime minister, after the first general election in 1991, was unwilling to hold an election, a fact which had come to public knowledge. The reason for avoiding an election was its influence on the sharing of power. Decentralisation, which had already advanced considerably, was not very compatible with the absolute control of the party in power. In the past politicians who had needed centralisation of power to remain in power had always had conflicts and confrontations with the local institutions of self-governance. Local units aggregate local interests and opinions and give them effective expression. These units occasionally come into conflict with centralised political parties. Particularly, the party in power wanted nominated political workers to serve as carriers of the messages of the government, whereas the leaders of local government representatives, enjoying the trust and confidence of the people, passed the legitimate messages of the people to the government. Party units depended on the will of leaders, whereas the leaders of elected local units were demanding and very assertive because they had grassroots support. The central government was usually composed of a homogeneous leadership, whereas most local units were either non-ideological or coalitions of more than one party. Most of the four thousand village units and thirty-six town units of self-government had political combinations in the executive committees as well as in the assemblies. The general pattern of local self-government was coalitions, so a situation of reconciliation was evolved to address the heterogeneity of interests and ideologies. Incidentally, the central government was forced to reflect upon the same sort of coalition due to the result of the recent election.

The 1990 Constitution brought a major change in the matter of representation. As the basic structure of the Constitution, adult franchise, a parliamentary system of government and multiparty democracy had to be accomplished along with constitutional monarchy. Under the 1990 Constitution Parliament consisted of His Majesty and two houses. The House of Representative consisted of 205 members elected by direct adult franchise. The Upper House consisted of 60 members from different channels. Ten members of the Upper House were nominated by the king from among people with good reputations in society or who had made prominent contributions to various fields of national life. Thirty-five members, including three women, were elected by the members of the House of Representatives on the basis of proportional representation by means of a single transferable vote. Fifteen members, three from each of the five development regions, were elected on the basis of the system of single transferable vote by different units of local self-government. The whole organisation of the upper house of parliament was aimed towards synthesising and reconciling with different sectors of interests and opinions. By Article 46 (1) (C), it became mandatory to constitute local units of representation and hold periodic elections to those bodies. By this provision of the Constitution alone, Nepal continued with five development regions. This clause almost provided continuity despite the otherwise drastic change in the representation in the House of Representatives.

The first two general elections under the multiparty system, held in 1991 and 1994 respectively, were assessed to be generally free and fair by various observation groups, which included persons from various countries. In both elections, the percentage of voters was higher than expected: 65 percent in 1991 and 62 percent in 1994. These rates were considered generally satisfactory. Except for a few cases of violence, polling was largely peaceful throughout the country. Election expenditures appeared high, but big money did not ensure success in the election. Defeat of the party in power proved that neither the use nor the misuse of government power affected the result of the election very much. No political party had an effective machinery to win the election by using irregular means, even if it wished to.

A number of political parties were also in the process of elimination. Before the election, many political parties fought for election symbols, which, following a Supreme Court decision, were allotted to whatever party applied for them. The

1990 Constitution had a provision for political organisations. Under Article 113, political parties or organisations wishing to get recognition from the Election Commission for the purpose of election had to procure more than three percent of the total votes cast in the election for the House of Representatives. In the 1991 parliamentary election, only five political parties were able to secure more than three per cent of the total votes polled and in the 1994 election, only four political parties managed to secure more than that threshold. Even among these four, two political parties were able to get a much higher percentage than others, mainly because of the first-past-the-post election system, in which minority votes were wasted. Knowing the trend of the results, voters generally chose candidates who had a chance not only to win but also to provide an alternative government.

A first-past-the-post system of election comes to a deadlock when a particular political party emerges without a viable government, as occurred during the first parliamentary election in 1958. In the 109-member House of Representatives, Nepali Congress had a two-thirds majority with 74 seats and the main opposition party, Gorkha Dal, had 18 seats. The Communist Party of Nepal at that time had four seats only. In the 1991 parliamentary election, the Nepali Congress had a simple majority, and the Communist Party of Nepal (Unified Marxist Leninist) had a powerful presence. In the 205-member house, the Nepali Congress party had 114 seats and CPN-UML had 69 seats. In that election, Nepali Congress secured about 37 per cent of the popular votes and CPN-UML had about 29 per cent. Voting figures did not give the same results. By getting about 37 per cent of votes in 1958, the Nepali Congress party was able to get two-thirds of the seats in the House of Representatives. About the same percentage of votes gave this party a slight majority in 1991. In the 1994 election, the recipient of the largest number of votes was Nepali Congress, which had about 33 per cent, followed by the CPN-UML, which formed the government by receiving the largest number of seats with about 30 per cent of the votes. The emergence of a third political party with a substantial number of seats in the parliament was an unexpected situation in the election system adopted by the country. The justification of the first-past-the-post election system was that it would provide a strong and stable government. However, the result of the 1994 election forced the creation of an unstable coalition government, a situation for which no party was mentally prepared. Thus, Nepal had a minority government that had uncertain prospects with regard to securing the support of other big parties. People were afraid there would be another election soon if the desired consensus failed to emerge.

The election system which was adopted for the House of Representatives in the 1990 Constitution works smoothly in a two-party system, but the emergence of three or more parties cannot be restricted by law. Even in developed democracies, sometimes a two-party system faces such crisis. When David Owen formed the Social Democratic Party in the United Kingdom, for example, worries were expressed about the stability of the government. Similarly, the candidature of Ross Perot as a very serious independent standing against the two main parties in the United States of America, the Democrats and Republicans, was seen as a crisis in the two-party system. The Economist discusses the views of several scholars to find a solution to this problem, which occasionally emerges in two-party systems. Citing American examples, it states:

> Two big obstacles stand in the way. One is the desperate, incoherent nature of voters' discontent. A large number of Americans know that they are dissatisfied with the choice offered by the two major parties, but they are less sure what they want instead. No alternative party has yet come up with a programme to match them. An even bigger obstacle is the first-past-the-post system for Congress, which makes it especially hard for fledgling parties to gain seats and grow.

Accepting that approach, Nepal's 1994 election results can be described as a reflection of the voters' dissatisfaction with the ruling Nepali Congress party and their support for more than one alternative. The divided mood of the people forced a coalition or a consensus government because, in a democracy, the verdict of the sovereign people is always respected as right. As three major parties were competing for survival in a system suitable mainly for just two parties in its usual course, voters, as consumers, offered the option of preserving two by eliminating the third. Another significant trend in the election regarded the voters' formation of a broad national outlook in choosing their representatives. In a multi-ethnic, multi-lingual nation such as Nepal, voters reflected a non-parochial choice. In Nepal's traditional society, the victory of the Communist Party of Nepal itself was evidence of the people's non-traditional approach to politics.

A democratic method of representation in the government has a positive impact on the functioning of political parties. Earlier there were a large number of Communist organisations advocating a dictatorship of the proletariat through a violent revolution though Nepal had no such class system as is found in an industrialised nation. Soon after the general election in 1991 when the Communists emerged as the main opposition party in Parliament with a substantial number of seats, they adopted a resolution in their party congress declaring their faith in multiparty democracy. In a competition with many other factions of Communists, CPN-UML emerged as the mainstream Communist Party in Nepal. It contested the parliamentary election in 1991 by a call for a government of workers and peasants, but its slogan in the 1994 election was a government of nationalists and democrats. As the prospect for getting into power through ballot became greater, there was a marked change in their style as well as their rhetoric, a change which gave them the fruits of power. Some ministers and members of parliament in that party have been convicted of crimes against their "class enemies". But since they were in power, there was no protest against them in the country.

Similarly, people who had helped the king to switch over to the panchayat system by rejecting multiparty parliamentary democracy emerged as a third force in Parliament in the name of the Rashtriya Prajatantra Party. The party's chairman, Surya Bahadur Thapa, was a prominent minister after the royal takeover in 1960 and led the partyless panchayat to victory in the 1980 national referendum, too. In the 1994 election, he emerged as the popularly elected leader of a democratic party functioning in an exemplary manner. His success in running the party better than others may be due to his and other party members' long experience in power during the panchayat regime, with due compromise and concession. The Panchas re-emergence as democrats is testimony to their political training through various democratic institutions under the panchayat system. It is strange that the Nepali Congress, a party of avowed democrats engaged in a long struggle failed to complete a full term in the government despite their having a workable majority in Parliament mainly due to the members' continual internal bickering. They did to themselves what the combined opposition in the parliament had failed to do when a no-confidence motion was tabled in the winter session of the parliament in 1994.

Other political parties, too, were forced to change their earlier postures and style of functioning by the competitive and representative political situation of the country. Actually, political parties are still in the process of democratising themselves. There were both ideological and non-ideological political parties in the country. But in a new national as well as international environment, all political parties have a non-ideological tendency. Therefore, to appeal to voters during election campaigns and to the people in general, non-ideological programmes were offered by all parties of significant standing. All major political parties have similar views on economic liberalisation, privatisation and open government. All major parties also support the basic norms of the 1990 Constitution, even during the election, as is reflected in their election manifestos. This consensus about the 1990 Constitution is a great assurance for a developing democracy like Nepal.

In the functioning of the first parliament under the 1990 Constitution, people observed the performances of various parties very minutely, as the results of the election suggest. Parliament as a whole was quite successful in drawing the attention of the people to the vital affairs of the state. The government and the opposition engaged in tough fights over issues like a treaty with India on the sharing of water resources, especially with regard to the Tanakpur Treaty; privatisation policies; the flow of foreign immigrants, especially from India; and the tilt towards India on various issues, a situation which taught people to give their verdicts through the ballot. The change of government in this way has generated faith among a people who had recent memories of a system in which it was much too difficult to challenge the status quo. It is generally seen that people are encouraged to follow extra-legal and non-peaceful courses to find a remedy to such a state. Whenever a remedy works effectively, however, even parties that once preached violent revolution and dictatorship start appealing for reconciliation and consensus. Recent political events in Nepal have sufficiently testified to this fact.

A great deal of controversy arose in the ruling CPN-UML party as to whether the elected members of the parliament should abide by the discipline of the leader of the parliamentary party or whether they should follow the dictates of the central body of leadership of the party, most of whose members were not elected. The prime minister had the backing of the popular election to implement his programmes, but the central bodies of the party asserted their position of overall leadership. Besides, the Nepali Congress, which held the government from 1991 to 1994, had a non-elected and non-statutory position of a "supreme leader", who very much believed that the party as well as the parliamentary unit of the party should follow his dictates because he had better knowledge of the heart and pulse of the common people than other party members. As a result, the party was not able to function in parliament efficiently or to build up the organisation to face new political challenges when the Nepali Congress was elected to power to deliver services to the people to whom they had promised a lot. For the people, the Nepali Congress representatives proved to be untrustworthy and for the party, they proved to be disorganised. The controversy regarding the supremacy of leadership between the central party body and the parliamentary body of the party remained unresolved even after the party's defeat in the 1994 election. Elected members of the party in parliament were going to elect a leader of the parliamentary party, but again the entrenched leadership of the party forced them to accept the leader of its choice. When democratic norms fail to work, traditional authority prevails. The Nepali Congress party could be a very interesting case for a study of a democratic party functioning in a traditional society with regard to the matter of popular representation. Its history is a record of struggle for democratic values, but it has been able to survive always under a patriarchal leadership. Parties with a less democratic image than Nepali Congress have actually functioned more democratically. Like a person, political parties as corporate bodies, also have some elements of individuality and character with which the society has to live. A popular political party embodies the character of a nation, too.

Nepal's 1990 Constitution was based on the principle of the separation of the powers of the state. Parliament represents the people. All executive functions face sanctions and derive legitimacy from parliamentary legislation. An independent judiciary, particularly the Supreme Court, dispenses justice not only according to law but also by its power to nullify laws through a process of judicial review. It was, therefore, not a system of strict parliamentary supremacy. Treaty-making power was to be exercised under parliamentary ratification according to Article 126 of the Constitution, but, at the same time, the Supreme Court had an established power of judicial review. A system of several checks and balances was a prominent feature of the Constitution. The violation of that system resulted in the punishment of the Nepali Congress party by voters in 1994.

In conclusion, Nepal, under the 1990 Constitution had a bi-cameral legislature through popular representation. The House of Representatives was elected on the basis of universal adult franchise in a single-member constituency, and the Upper House was constituted partly by the king's nomination following the advice of the prime minister and partly on the basis of indirect election from the local and district tiers of local self-government units. Thirty members of the Upper House were elected on the basis of proportional representation with single transferable system. The House of Representatives had an important role in choosing the prime minister and played a decisive role in passing legislation and ensuring on the accountability of the government. On many important issues, joint sessions of both houses were held. The ratification of treaties involving vital national interests required a joint session of the parliament. The Supreme Court ordered the government to ratify a controversial treaty with India, on the sharing of water resources related to the Tanakpur Barrage Project, but the government did not comply. It was a prominent issue raised by the opposition parties in the election, and it was one of the main reasons that the ruling Nepali Congress party lost the election. The fact that the entire term of parliament was full of public issues raised by the opposition parties educated the people to take political decisions as voters and citizens.

The other most important institutions of popular representation in Nepal were the units of local self-government. Starting three decades earlier, several elections had been held, a process which had educated the people to exercise their franchise as well as work with the executive and the assembly on a micro scale. Based on the traditional institution of the panchayat, democracy at the grassroots has social and cultural roots. These local units functioned as the lowest unit of government administration. After an adequate apprenticeship in the partyless system, political parties contested with mixed results, forcing them to enter in to an uneasy fray. In the absence of other effective functional groups, local units of self-government became the people's means of articulating and expressing their general will.

Political polarisation as a product of post-industrial democracies was experimented with during the pre-industrial and mainly traditional situation of Nepal, where there was no legacy of modernisation by an industrial power. Such polarisation started functioning in a pluralistic social and cultural background. As a result, parties, even those with fully democratic commitments, have not been able to function democratically in the modern world. Party members rarely got the opportunity to elect their leaders. The leaders were not accountable to the people. Party programmes were decided ad hoc without consulting members and members were expected to unquestioningly obey the dictates of leaders who were acting in the traditional style of a patriarch. It is under this political tradition that a party in the government was appealing for consensus support to continue in power despite its not having a majority.

For political leadership, people have an extensive network of political parties and a well-organised system of local self-government that have to co-exist in a traditional society depending mainly on a traditional agricultural economy. What industrialised democracies are practicing is being expected very fast and up to the mark in a basically rural environment characterised by rampant poverty and illiteracy, a fact which quickly frustrates impatient people. Progress toward the modern concept of democracy is so slow that people are tempted to jump into other untested alternatives, discarding the experiences of the past completely. That said, a society can hardly just get rid of its heritage. Political parties, therefore, have to learn to co-exist with many traditional institutions and adjust with democratically elected units of self-governments for leadership. We have yet to see political parties organising and managing themselves democratically.

The 1990 Constitution was quite favourable for a democratic and representative form of government. The Supreme Court has consistently functioned with extraordinary powers to provide remedies and serve as a final interpreter of the law since 1951. A very serious constitutional controversy was settled by the verdict of the Supreme Court regarding the dissolution of the House of Representatives on the recommendation of the prime minister. Though there has been some grumbling among a section of politicians, the people, in general, accepted its ruling in a democratic spirit. This was one of the greatest ordeals for the people in terms of new constitutional practice. A process of checks and balances and the accountability of the government were taken very seriously in the draft of the Constitution. If this principle appears not to be functioning, one has to see how people can be motivated and made responsive.

In its own tradition, Nepal is a unique model of compromise and reconciliation as well as change with continuity. It is a nation in which Communists are elected to rule in a multiparty democracy and the monarchy is respected as a symbol of nationalism and national unity through a consensus constitution. Democratic development has a favourable climate to progress unless it is again disturbed by extraneous circumstances.

References

Democratic Innovations in Nepal, Bhuwan L. Joshi *and* Leo E. Rose, University of California Press, 1966.

Heroes and Builders of Nepal, Rishikesh Shaha. Oxford University Press, 1970.

Prithwinarayan Shah in the Light of Dibya Upadesh, L.F. Stiller, S.J. Himalaya Book Centre, 1989.

India and Nepal: An Exercise in Open Diplomacy, Shriman Narayan. Orient Paperbacks, New Delhi, 1971.

The Economist, London. November 5, 1994.

Towards Revolution, Jayaprakash Narayan. Arnold-Heinemann Publishers (India), 1975.

Kanoon (magazine), Number 12, Nepal Kitab Company, Kathmandu.

Nepal: Profile of a Himalayan Kingdom, Leo E. Rose and John T. Scholz, Select Service Syndicate, New Delhi, 1980.

II

The Right to Work and Economic Development in Nepal

Within the purview of the general theme for discussion, I shall deal specifically with a citizen's right to work and right to economic development under the law of Nepal. Countries in South Asia which have a great number of dissimilarities and disparities have aligned themselves to promote their mutual interests on the basis of sovereign equality and equitable cooperation. Strategically located between Central and South Asia, Nepal was motivated to join the democratically organised community of nations of South Asia to expand its friendly relations and to meet the challenges of economic development. A gathering like this, the Third SAARC Law Conference, I believe, may help enhance our mutual and deep understanding of each other's problems and help us evolve a common legal approach to tackle the problems that we all share as well as those that are unique to each of us.

Nepal does not yet have much experience in the area of labour legislation. Economically, it is in the pre-industrial stage, whereas most of its neighbouring countries in South

Asia shared knowledge of and experiences in labour legislation with a highly industrialised nation when they were under colonial rule. The situation in Nepal is unique in many respects because it has always maintained itself as a sovereign, independent nation. Although landlocked, it was never subjected to the colonial rule. Its citizens have the greatest of reputation for bravery even though they live amidst abject poverty. Although Nepal enjoyed two centuries of friendship with highly industrialised Britain, it did not import modern technology or improve access to the English language. Nepal has its own native language which serves as the lingua franca within the nation, but this fact makes dialogue with the people of other countries of the region challenging. Despite these constraints, the indigenously developed legal system of Nepal translated and incorporated many provisions of foreign laws ahead of its time.

Nepal was successful in resisting the expansion of empire by both its northern and southern neighbours. It preserved its independence in isolation. Traditionally, it has a subsistence economy. The rapid decolonisation of countries around it following the termination of World War II forced drastic changes in Nepal, too. After some trial and error with several earlier constitutions, Nepal promulgated its fifth constitution in 1990 with the goal of achieving all three generations of human rights, including the right to economic development. It is said that the first generation of rights emerged from the American and French revolutions; the second generation of rights with the Russian Revolution, which culminated in welfare concepts; and the third generation of rights was in response to global interdependence, which necessitated the right to economic development.

In the present legal set up, Nepal has more promise than practical experience in labour legislation and liberal economic agendas. Within the parameters of the present constitution, efforts are being made to catch up with the pace of development in the rest of the countries in South Asia. The results so far are not very encouraging due to certain harsh realities. A broad national consensus, however, has been accommodated in the 1990 Constitution, which begins by stating that the first objective of "the sovereign and independent Nepal" was to safeguard the independence and sovereignty of the nation. The second most important objective was the consolidation of multiparty democracy and constitutional monarchy. The third objective was economic in nature and included a citizen's right to work and the people's right to economic development. Both the growth of democratic institutions and of the economy has to be achieved within a short period to ensure the twin goals of guaranteeing the freedom of citizens and safeguarding the independence of the nation.

The constitution lays out the basic social and economic commitments of the state under two sections, "Directive Principles" and "State Policy". One of the main objectives of the state is to establish "a just system in all aspects of national life, including social, economic and political life." The directive principles lay down that "the fundamental objective of the state shall be to transform the national economy into an independent and self-reliant system by preventing the available resources and means of the country from being concentrated within a limited section of the society by making arrangements for the equitable distribution of economic gains on the basis of social justice, by making such provisions as well to prevent economic exploitation of any class or individual, and by giving preferential treatment and encouragement to national enterprises, both private and public."

Having enshrined the right to work in the directive principles, the state is committed "to preserve a policy of increasing participation of the labour force, the chief socio-economic force of the country, in the management of enterprises by gradually securing employment opportunities to it ensuring the right to work and thus protecting its rights and interest." The constitution also guarantees the "freedom to practice any profession, or to carry on any occupation, industry or trade" as a fundamental right. This guarantee was lacking in previous constitutions. Likewise, the right against exploitation as a fundamental right is elaborated as below:

> Right against exploitation: (1) Traffic in human beings, slavery, serfdom or forced labour in any form is prohibited. Any contravention of this provision shall be punishable by law. Provided that nothing herein shall be a bar to providing by law for compulsory service for public purposes. (2) No minor shall be employed to work in any factory or mine or be engaged in any other hazardous work.

The Constitution has guaranteed the fundamental right to a constitutional remedy for the enforcement of all fundamental rights. The government is under obligation to get the legal system restructured in the spirit of the constitution. The Supreme Court, as the custodian of the rights of the people, reviews laws contrary to the Constitution. The Supreme Court's judgement on labour legislation has wide implications as it declared a provision of the Labour Act ultra vires to the constitution and upheld the citizen's right to work. Before discussing the implications of the verdict, a brief discussion of Nepal's labour legislation is appropriate.

Till 1959, the Civil Code (Mulki Ain) had a general provision regarding labour and wages. It made it mandatory to pay wages to persons who rendered their work unless the agreement was otherwise. In 1959, the first comprehensive labour law was enacted, the Factory and Factory Workers Act. This act had adequate provisions regarding working conditions, health, sanitation, security, working hours, welfare schemes, wage regulations and regulation of alien workers. Workers had the right to strike as part of their right to organise for collective bargaining. Management also had the power to block the establishment of unions on certain grounds. In other industrial democracies, such labour legislation was the outcome of the serious and organised struggle of the working class, whereas all the basic facilities for workers in Nepal were introduced without any such struggle.

There was a labour movement in 1940s under the leadership of Girija Prasad Koirala. However, the country never had a strong labour organisation. There were complaints from a segment of the population in India against Nepal's work permit system, which was introduced in 1988. This opposition was one of the issues behind India's economic blockade against Nepal in 1989.

After the momentous political changes in April 1990, the Factory and Factory Workers Act 1959 was replaced by the Labour Act 1992, which was not substantially different from the previous act except for those provisions relating to foreign workers. Although the 1959 Act was completely silent on foreign workers, a clause included in the Act in effect allowed foreign workers to compete with Nepali citizens without the prior permission of the government department. According to one provision, Nepali citizens would get preference in any appointment. No organised union of workers spoke out against this provision as its effect was not properly understood. Another clause in the 1992 Act says that workers get a permanent appointment after completing a one-year probation. Even a foreign worker becomes eligible for permanent appointment, a provision that the Act did not prohibit under Nepal's citizenship law. Aliens who reside in Nepal continuously for 15 years become eligible for citizenship. A recent change in the citizenship law, which was challenged at the Supreme Court (which had yet to give its judgement at the time of writing this paper) is that a person can claim citizenship if he has permanent employment in any government-owned corporation. Thus, the 1992 Act, which seems to be dealing with factory workers alone, has wider implications for the acquisition of citizenship. Since citizens constitute the people and the nation and are where the sovereignty of Nepal rests, this Act, has wider implications for the sovereignty of Nepal.

This provision of the 1992 Labour Act was challenged in the Supreme Court under a public interest litigation by lawyer Bal Krishna Neupane. The government defended the provision of the Act with a plea that for the rapid development of the country, foreign workers were necessary in those services in which trained Nepalis were not available. The Supreme Court found that the Constitution itself discriminated between Nepal's citizens and foreigners. The freedom to practice any profession and carry on any occupation, industry or trade is guaranteed only to citizens. In the opinion of the Court, to treat equals as unequals and unequals as equals goes against the right to equality guaranteed to citizens. The Industrial Enterprises Act 1992, which was promulgated soon after the Labour Act 1992, has a provision stating that the prior consent of the government be sought before inviting a foreigner for a job. Conditions stipulated in the Industrial Enterprises Act were not included in the Labour Act. The Supreme Court, in its reasoned decision, declared the unreasonable clause of the Labour Act as ultra vires. The government issued a rule under the Labour Act 1992 abiding by the decision of the Supreme Court. The existing position of the law in Nepal does not allow foreign workers to be appointed in the informal sector of industry without the permission of the government for an appointment to be permanent. Under the Labour Rule 1993, a foreign worker can be appointed to an enterprise with the consent of the Labour Department at the recommendation of the Labour Officer only if Nepali citizens are not available for the job. Such appointments can be made for a period not exceeding two years. Management which employs a foreign national is also required to train a Nepali replacement for the job.

Despite the legal constraints, foreign workers in Nepal have been great beneficiaries in the formal sector of the economy, and their total number in other sectors, especially the informal sector of the economy, is alarmingly high. In their study of the labour situation in Nepal, two noted economists, Biswambhar Pyakuryal and Narendra Bhattarai, released interesting findings:

Size of industry	Percentage of industries employing foreign manpower	
	Direct	Indirect
Large	55%	35%
Medium	50%	55%
Cottage & Small	2%	10%

The percentages presented in the above table relate only to formal-sector industries, where, incidentally, less than three percent of Nepal's population is engaged. Although no study has been carried out, it has been estimated that foreigners working in the informal sector of the economy total roughly 6.5 million. Nepal's present population is 18 million. If the present rate of population growth continues, the population is expected to double in 27 years. By the year 2030, Nepal is expected to have a population of at least 32.4 million. Per capita income declined from USD 180 in 1991 to USD 170 in 1992, according to the World Bank Atlas 1993, which makes Nepal the poorest country in the world. Within the present decade, job opportunities have to be created for half a million workers annually to benefit Nepalis alone. The illiteracy rate is 36 per cent but at least 50,000 graduates do not have jobs, not even as schoolteachers. Just to sustain the present living standard, the economic growth rate will have to increase by at least 4 per cent. Most foreign workers come from a country in which 55 million people are unemployed. This unemployment figure alone is three times Nepal's entire population. If Nepal continues to keep the door open for all, the Nepalese will be left with no jobs in their own country. The Nepali state has made a commitment in the Constitution to provide employment opportunities so that its citizens can exercise their right to work.

Considering the size and the capacity of the country, it is not possible to maintain a free flow of immigrant workers in the region. Every state has a commitment first to its citizens. This fact does not mean the absolute denial of employment to all foreign workers. Countries in the process of industrial development may need a large workforce from other countries. Among European countries, the workforce of Austria, which has a population the size of Nepal's, comprises 10 per cent of foreign workers.

Malaysia only recently said it would need at least one million workers, workers it is seeking from Indonesia. It seems that at present, every country in the region has surplus labour. Given that this is the situation, the entry of foreign workers has to be properly regulated. Unregulated immigrant labourers tend to settle permanently and demand citizenship. Nepal is under tremendous strain to deal with unregulated immigrants from one particular country, a fact which has endangered its demographic situation. Dr. Kishore K. Guru-Gharana puts the problem thus:

> The movement of people from India to Nepal for economic as well as socio-cultural reasons is almost equal in size to the total population growth per year (around 2.5 per cent of population of Nepal). In the case of India, however, the cross-border movement from Nepal would amount to 0.05 per cent of its population. In fact, population growth of India is nearly equal to the total population of Nepal. Therefore, the weight of this population control aspect of regional cooperation hinges on the sympathy and understanding on the part of India toward the high significance attached to this matter by its small neighbour. The insistence on reciprocity in this matter would not be in the spirit of closer cooperation since the states involved are so significantly different.

The Nepalese had favoured treatment in India till the British Rule. In 1950, a treaty was signed by the governments of Nepal and India giving national-like treatment on the basis of reciprocity. But on the same date of the signing, a letter was exchanged by the same authorities who suspended the operation of the reciprocity clause by another clause, which read like this: "it may be necessary for some time to come to afford the Nepali nationals in Nepal from unrestricted competition." Mutual agreement on the implementation of this provision was reflected on several occasions and through various means. In a parliamentary debate on this issue, India's Prime Minister Jawaharlal Nehru in 1952 explained: "Because of conditions in Nepal, we do not want to press the Nepalis to open the door to everybody." In 1966, this understanding was reiterated by Dinesh Singh, the foreign minister of India. This equitable stand did not remain consistent. Nepal-India relations reached the most critical phase ever in 1988, during which period the question of discrimination against Indian citizens in Nepal was also raised. Work permits, which mainly affected Indian workers, were opposed. There was a great political upheaval in 1989 during a serious economic impasse between Nepal and India. Indeed, India's unilateral trade blockade ultimately brought a drastic change in the political system and the form of the government in Nepal.

Soon after assuming the office of the prime minister in the interim coalition government, Krishna Prasad Bhattarai visited India in June 1990 to renegotiate the Transit Treaty. India insisted on settling the entire gamut of issues in the relations between the two countries. There was a detailed proposal from India which would have changed the independent identity of Nepal, as Mr. Bhattarai revealed in a public disclosure during his campaign for a bye-election in 1993. What actually transpired between the two prime ministers in New Delhi is not fully known. At the end of the official talks, Nepal and India issued a joint communiqué covering trade, transit, water resources and the granting of national-like treatment to Indians in Nepal. Nepal was asked to exempt Indian nationals from the ambit of the work permit scheme, and Indian nationals employed as teachers in schools in Nepal were to be put on the same footing as Nepalis with regard to the terms and conditions of their employment. As the prime minister had a limited mandate in the interim period, this part of the understanding was not pursued. Nepal maintained its legal position outside of a short-lived deviation under the Labour Act which has now been corrected by the Supreme Court. Nepal has been experiencing great hardship since March 1987, when India unilaterally terminated the Transit Treaty. An unjust and unequal treaty with a hint of coercion can hardly be justified by the progressive principles of international law. Such progressive principles should be the basis for Nepal's relations with its neighbours.

Worries are being expressed in Nepal regarding the increasing number of unregulated foreign workers. Dr. Devendra Raj Pandey, a noted economist who served as the finance minister in the interim coalition government and accompanied Mr. Bhattarai to New Delhi, ignoring what was imposed on foreign workers, said:

> Personally, I am more disturbed by Indian worker's unrestricted entry into Nepal. My apprehension is justified even on the basis of the norms followed globally in respect of the movement of labour. Liberalisation or not, immigration laws are being changed around the world to restrict such movements. Where we need to worry, therefore, is how we convince India that it has to abide by the principles of non-reciprocity in the movement of labour whereby the opportunities available to Nepalis for work in India is not linked with the movement of Indian labour in Nepal. If we can work this out, Nepal may not need any specified trade preferences in India.

It is to be regretted that these people missed an opportunity to pursue India then, when it had a new leadership and when there was also a tremendous amount of goodwill for Nepal after the restoration of multiparty democracy. The regressive 1992 Labour Act was the outcome of this missed opportunity. However, the legal status of workers has come into proper shape since the Supreme Court declared the provision which treated Nepali nationals on par with Indian nationals as ultra vires after it was immediately challenged in the court. As long as there are two separate and independent countries, the citizens of one country will be foreigners in the other. The constitutions of both countries discriminate between a citizen and a foreign national. Thus, a citizen's right to work was protected by the Supreme Court. On the issue of discriminating between a citizen and a foreigner, Benjamin Cardozo in a decision in 1915 said: "To disqualify aliens is discrimination, indeed, but not an arbitrary discrimination, for the principles of exclusion is the restriction of the resources of the state, ungenerous and unwise such discrimination may be, it is not for that reason unlawful."

International relations enriched by the experiences of two World Wars have advanced progressively. But the basic themes of national interests and economic nationalism remain prime considerations. Paul Kennedy, in his *Preparing for the Twenty-First Century*, visualises future trends thus:

> With population pressures building up in various parts of the globe, the struggle for resources intensifying, and the communications revolution often fueling ethnic animosities rather than producing world citizens, the challenge to national authority—especially in the poorest parts of the world, may intensify. ... There may have been certain erosion of powers of the nation-state in recent decades, but

> the nation-state remains the primary locus of identity of most people; regardless of who their employers is and what they do for a living, individuals pay taxes to the state, are subjected to its laws, serve (if need be) in its passport. ... The global demographic explosion, atmospheric pollution, and technology driven change each have their own transnational momentum, which decide whether to abolish currency controls, permit, biotechnology, cut factory emissions or support a population policy.

The concepts of the rights of a person and the rights of a nation have had a progressive and positive contribution in the development of human rights and self-determination. There is an increasing demand for the rule of law, justice and equity in international relations. Under the auspices of the United Nations, the small and resourceless countries of the world have obtained the right to nationhood and self-determination on the basis of sovereign equality. The United Nations General Assembly Resolution of 1962 on Permanent Sovereignty over Natural Resources envisages "the creation and strengthening of the inalienable sovereignty of States over their natural wealth and resources" to reinforce "their economic independence." The Charter of Economic Rights and Duties of States lays down the principle that "every state has and shall freely exercise full permanent sovereignty, including possession, use and disposal, over all its wealth, natural resources and economic activities." The Declaration on the Establishment of a New International Economic Order promotes the transfer of technology with a right to economic self-determination. A resolution in 1979 emphasises that "the right to development is as much a prerogative of nations as of individuals within nations." A UN resolution relating to the Declaration on the Right to Development states that development is an inalienable human right and that equality of opportunity for development is the prerogative of both nations and the individuals who comprise them. Accordingly, the right to development also implies the full realisation of the right of all peoples to self-determination, which includes, subject to the relevant provisions of both international covenants on human rights, the exercise of their inalienable right to full sovereignty over all their natural wealth and resources. Nepal is a signatory to the International Covenant on Economic, Social and Cultural Rights as well as the International Covenant on Civil and Political Rights. Article 2.3 of ICESCR says that "developing countries, with due regard to human rights and their national economy, may determine to what extent they would guarantee the economic rights recognised in the present Covenant to non-nationals." Nepal, which has never been under alien rule, supported a UN resolution, "Granting Independence to Colonial Rule," denouncing "colonialism in all its forms and manifestations." A long list of such international charters and documents could be mentioned to confirm the sovereign right of every nation to determine its economic interests.

In light of these developments, it is clear that Nepal has an inalienable right to exercise its permanent sovereignty over its economic activities. In exercising its right to self-preservation, it has to protect citizens from unreasonable competition from foreign workers. To maintain reciprocal national treatment with a country whose population is 40 times its own is not only inequitable but also flouts the principle of self-preservation, which, irrespective of any unjust and unequal treaty, is inalienable. The free flow of immigrant workers is not possible in the region in the near future. Two or more countries of equal size, however, could treat each other's citizens like nationals. All countries of SAARC are nearby India, which has 77 per cent of the region's entire population. Any number of immigrant workers in India from the neighbouring countries would be insignificant whereas the demographic position and political situation of India's neighbours could be imbalanced with even an insignificant number of immigrants from India. In such a situation, instead of reciprocity, an equitable approach to immigrant workers is necessary to harmonise relations between the countries of the region.

On the issue of the New Economic Agenda, Nepal's 1990 Constitution lays down parameters and guidance. The state in Nepal has some economic commitments in order to secure for its citizens the right to economic development, which is highly valued by the world community as a third-generation human right. According to the directive principles of the Constitution, the fundamental objective of the state shall be to ensure that the national economy is independent and self-reliant. The modes to achieve these objectives are specified in the Constitution. It declares that the available resources and means of the country should not be concentrated within a limited section of the society. The state has an obligation to make arrangements for the equitable distribution of economic gains on the basis of social justice. In addition, preferential treatment and encouragement are to be given to the national enterprises, both private and public. Under the state policy declared by the Constitution, the state shall, for the purposes of national development, take measures necessary to attract foreign capital and technology while, at the same time, promoting indigenous investment. Being the latest democratic document, the 1990 Constitution avoids the extremes of socialism and laissez-faire. Foreign private investment and the transfer of technology should help and promote national economic development.

Since the promulgation of the 1990 Constitution, the economy of the country has been getting a new shape under the declared policy of the government to privatise public sector enterprises and leave the economy to function in a competitive free market economy. The ruling political party included democratic socialism in its election manifesto, but, in practice, even the principles of a mixed economy are being discarded. What is desired in the Constitution is not found in policy. A brief account of recent experiences will help reach a conclusion on the discrepancies between ideological commitment and actual practice.

The restoration of multiparty democracy in Nepal was definitely a watershed event in many respects. The economic impasse with India persisted. Nepal was able to manage its trade on the basis of a most favoured nation and with the help of an open general license system after the termination of the trade and transit treaties. As the country has access to the sea mainly through India, the termination of the treaty with India seriously affected its third-country trade. During the Indian blockade, the diesel needed to complete one of the country's biggest hydroelectric projects had to be air-lifted from Bangladesh. In this situation, an all-party agitation was concluded with a compromise which not only changed the politicians in the government but also changed the very form of government itself.

The first and foremost task of the interim government was to negotiate a trade as well as a transit treaty with India. Following the restoration of multiparty democracy, Nepal had very high expectations for support and sympathy, especially from democratic countries. A permanent, convenient and economic transit was its minimum expectation. During the British regime in India, Nepal had a permanent transit facility, but that was made periodical, up for renewal every five years, after a treaty in 1950. It is impractical for Nepal to plan for long-term economic development with such a short-term transit facility. During each and every negotiation of the transit facility, Nepal has been compelled to agree on terms unfavourable to its national interests. The temporary nature of the transit facility has always put Nepal at an economic disadvantage and subjected it to economic coercion. Treatment of the newly emerged democratic set-up and the government of Nepal were no more liberal than they had been in the past. Interim Prime Minister Bhattarai succumbed to the following pressure to get a temporary transit facility:

1. Tariff preferences for Indian goods by, inter alia, exemption of additional customs duty, will be restored.
2. Primary products imported from India will be exempt from basic customs duty, as is the case for similar products from Nepal imported to India.
3. Tariff preferences for third-country goods should not be detrimental to the tariff regime for India.
4. The valuation of Indian goods exported under DPR for assessment of basic customs duty will be made on the basis of ex-factory-depot price, excluding any element of refundable Indian duties and taxes, but including transport and insurance charges, wherever applied.
5. Indian nationals will be removed from the ambit of the work permit scheme.
6. Indian nationals employed in schools in Nepal will be placed on the same footing as Nepali nationals with regard to terms and conditions of employment.

7. Removal of restrictions on the movement of Indian currency between Nepal and India on the basis of reciprocity.
8. Restoration of facilities for Indian nationals to have their vehicles registered in Nepal on the basis of reciprocity.

The two prime ministers issued a joint communiqué reiterating their respect for the principles of sovereign equality, territorial integrity, national independence, non-use of force, non-interference in each other's affairs and peaceful settlement of all disputes. They also agreed to respect each other's security concerns and to have prior consultation with a view to reaching mutual agreement on defence-related matters which, in view of either country, could pose a threat to its security. Nepal's permanent sovereignty over its natural resources was compromised "for the harnessing of the waters of the common rivers for the benefit of the two peoples and for the protection and management of the environment."

Because of its landlocked situation, Nepal has always had weak bargaining power. In spite of the great support for the cause of democracy in Nepal, the above-mentioned terms of agreement reflect the hardship the country faces in its efforts to secure economic progress. Since rivers are Nepal's main natural resource for any kind of economic development, the imposed concept of a common river has deprived Nepal of its freedom to harness its rivers. In December 1993, an action plan agreed between the two countries included three more major river projects in Nepal under the principle of common river. Both countries agreed to complete the projects on a bilateral basis and with funding to be mobilised from multilateral agencies. A clause in the action plan permits Nepal to have priority in the consumption of the water in its own sovereign territory. This was a typical example of an unequal and inequitable agreement imposed upon a small, poor and landlocked country. Explaining the importance of the principle of permanent sovereignty over natural resources, Kamal Hussain, a Saudi Arabian representative, said the following: "It is indeed to prevent what had been a frequent occupancy in the nineteenth century, namely that weak and penniless governments, should seriously compromise a country's future by granting concessions in the economic sphere." He also mentioned the inequitable and onerous arrangements imposed during the colonial era: "The asymmetry of concession type arrangement between host government and transnational corporations, resulting from inequality in bargaining power and lack of negotiating capability, continued even after countries became politically independent. Newly independent developing states lacked capital, technological knowhow and marketing capacity. Transnational corporations and other foreign investors could thus use their superior bargaining position to secure '*concessions*' or concessional-type arrangements. These gave them extensive control over operations, including the power to take critical decisions on matters such as the levels of investment, production and pricing. The host state under such arrangements remained the passive recipient of certain, often modest, financial benefits in the form of royalties and taxes."

The development of international law in the post-decolonisation era has yet to come into practice as a minimum standard of relations between countries with dissimilar situations. As mentioned by Subrata Roy Chowdhury, quoting the eminent Uruguyuan jurist Eduardo Jiminéz de Aréchega, the description of the right to full sovereignty as permanent indicates "that the territorial state can never lose its legal capacity to change the destination or the method of exploitation and administration." Aréchega further concludes that this right can be exercised "even if a predecessor state or a previous government engaged itself by treaty or by a contract not to do." Brownlie expressed the same opinion when he said that "permanent sovereignty is the assertion of the acquired rights of the host state which are not defensible by contract or perhaps even by international law stand in test in the context of Nepal."

Nepal is moving from a traditional to a modern industrialised economy. Nepal began to implement the Eighth Five-Year Plan in 1992, giving high priority to increasing the participation of the private sector, foreign investment and joint collaboration. The policy stated in the plan is to encourage foreign investment in order to promote foreign capital, modern technology, management and technical skills in the domestic industries, among others. The basic objectives of the plan were as follows:

1. Create additional income and employment opportunities by enhancing the inter-relationship between the production-oriented industrial sector and the other economic activities of the nation.
2. Develop the export sector as an important source to earn foreign exchange by enhancing production, productivity and the quality of exportable items.
3. Establish import substitutions by promoting cottage and small-scale industries as well as other industries to meet domestic demands.

4. Create necessary infrastructure for the use of mineral resources of the country which have the potential for commercial exploitation.
5. Increase national production through the development of industries based on existing mineral deposits.

Here is a critical assessment of public sector enterprises in favour of privatisation in that plan: "Public sector enterprises were established in Nepal with a view to provide and expand infrastructural services, to produce and deliver necessary consumer essentials, to create employment opportunities, to increase government revenue and to contribute to national development. A total of 62 public enterprises have been established. Despite a long period of protection, stated goals have not been achieved and the financial competence and abilities of public enterprises have deteriorated. Returns on investment have not only been minimal, but have also put great strains on government resources every year. It is now increasingly imperative to improve the performance of these corporations. In this regard, several public enterprises will be privatized in order to raise their competence and to improve their performance. Improvement and suitable rehabilitation programmes will be undertaken for corporations which will not be privatized or those that will be privatized later in order to enhance their performance." Various policies to complete the privatization processes are mentioned in the plan. One is that all policies and programmes relating to privatization will be transparent. That said, transparency is, in fact, the most significant thing missing in the process of privatisation in Nepal.

The government decided to privatise three major industries in the first phase, which was launched in 1992. None of these industries had been declared sick. The government may have believed that sick industries do not sell. These three industries were not only a gift from China but they also represented a transfer of technology from China to Nepal. They included brick and tile manufacturing with a unique technology, a leather and shoe factory, and a paper factory. In addition to technology, each industry had vast land assets worth more than the price of the industry itself. The price of the land was several times higher than that of the structures. A detailed description of the industries for privatisation was not duly published. In fact, buyers were more interested in the valuable land belonging to the industries than the industries themselves. The sale was not the privatisation of industries but the privatisation of valuable land.

The traditional pattern of investment in Nepal is mainly in immovable property, and, in the process of privatisation, factories were considered as junk in comparison to the land, which had a much higher commercial value than the price the buyers agreed to pay in easy installments. There was widespread criticism of this process of privatisation. Even the president of the ruling Nepali Congress party, K.P. Bhattarai, regretted that this privatisation did not fetch the price of the real estate the industries were on and that the national interests of Nepal were not given priority. Two of the three industries are under Indian management and the third is likely (at the time of writing) to follow suit as share holdings are changing substantially. People generally are apprehensive that the sale was not the privatisation but the 'foreignisation', or, more precisely, the 'Indianisation' of industries in Nepal. The foreign investment policy of the government admits there is an external factor in privatisation thus:

> The wave of change in the world economic order has affected all nations, big and small. In the process of adjusting the economy in line with these changes, neighbouring countries have also adopted an open and liberal policy for strengthening their economic systems. Accordingly, it is necessary for Nepal to introduce timely changes and reforms in various sectors of its economy to introduce dynamism in the process of economic development.

It is obvious that external influences were very much behind the process of privatisation in Nepal. In addition, a nexus of politicians, businesspeople and bureaucrats play an important role, as money plays a decisive role in power politics. Privatisation was not a well thought-out plan before it was launched. Nepal lacked the basic pre-conditions needed to make it beneficial. Industries were originally established in the public sector in Nepal because no private enterprises, either national or foreign, were prepared to assume the risks involved. Because it lacked conducive environment to implement socialist dogma. Nepal never had a bias for socialism in its economic planning even though politicians with socialist economic commitments had been in power. Privatisation was therefore introduced without the necessary preconditions and mainly as a dogma. Industrial growth in Nepal lacked the availability of basic infrastructures in transport and communication, both internal as well as external. Internal links and communication were difficult due to the rough geographical terrain. Externally, landlocked Nepal has always faced transit problems as the transit country has not accepted transit as the right of a landlocked country. The periodically negotiable short-term nature of the transit agreements discouraged long-term and big industrial ventures in Nepal. Senior economist Dr. Pyakuryal pointed out the challenge:

> Consideration of extending five-year limit of transit agreement with India would be important to convince foreign entrepreneurs for long term investment prospects in Nepal. An effort to review the pros and cons of trade and transit agreement with India in the context of economic liberalisation in both the countries can thus be considered to be another challenge in recent years.

Even when transit facilities are available, they are inconvenient and uneconomical. Nepali goods are transferred from seaports to its borders on a system that switches from broad-gauge to narrow-gauge railway tracks, a fact which causes considerable delays and pilferage. India's network of highly developed highways does not touch Nepal anywhere. Economical and convenient transportation of goods by big containers has not been possible. Given this situation, no one in Nepal can conceive of competing with the highly developed and organised industries of India, which have the advantage of a significantly more developed and bigger internal market. The above-mentioned conditions of the trade agreement clearly show that Nepal cannot adopt protective measures for its industries. In addition, Nepal cannot import goods from other countries, a practice which would be cheaper than importing them from India. Instead of protecting its own industries, Nepal has to follow protective measures for Indian industries. Transit is a favour India grants Nepal, but, in trade, Nepal has always sacrificed its interests in favour of those of India as a quid pro quo for these transit facilities. India's exports to other countries through hard currency are 30 per cent cheaper than its exports to Nepal, which are done mostly through Indian currency. Nepal's exports to India are subject to several tariff and non-tariff barriers, triggering fears that trade will be deflected despite the liberalisation of India's policy. The trade deficit with India has grown increasingly adverse, a fact which has forced Nepal to adjust its balance of payments with its surplus foreign exchange earnings from third-country trade. About 85 per cent of export earnings come to Nepal under a preferential trade facility provided by other countries. That amount of earning would not have been possible through traditional transit by land. Nepal has developed air links with many countries. Products such as woolen carpets, readymade garments and handicrafts are conveniently transported by air cargo even though it is expensive. Tribhuvan International Airport, the only international airport in Nepal, has a limited capacity and has already grown too congested since several private sector airlines started operating in the country.

Nepal was almost always an open, unrestricted and reserved market for Indian industries, but not a single big industrial investment was made by Indian industrialists in Nepal. None of the top ten industrialists in India, all of whom have invested in other countries of Asia and Africa, have shown any interest in Nepal, not even since Nepali governments since 1990 have adopted a great change in attitude towards India. None of the top ten industrial houses in India even took part in an international investment forum held in Kathmandu. The reasons are obvious. Any facility promised by Nepal is economically less attractive than options in India. Herein lies the crux of the problem which Nepal faces in its endeavour to achieve rapid economic development. Nepal is handicapped in spite of its hardworking people and generous friends, mainly because of the lack of permanent, economical and convenient transit as a matter of right, as provided for in international law.

The mere declaration of the government that it will uplift the economy through liberal, open and competitive policies and its drive to privatise a few public enterprises is not going to help much.

What is considered successful privatisation in Nepal is actually the privatisation of the real estate which public enterprises had owned. Under the pretext of privatisation, some easy money-making traders and merchants set their eyes on the real estate of public enterprises and the value of these assets has skyrocketed. Smuggling and easy money-making attracted a large number of traders and merchants from across the open border who live in Nepal without record or permission. The principle of privatisation has not been opposed in Nepal. Nor has foreign private investment. What is intriguing is the haste with which even profit-making public enterprises were handed over to inexperienced persons and foreigners without any consideration for the employment of Nepali nationals.

There was no privatisation act when the scheme was started. The Privatisation Act obtained royal assent in December 1993. It included a provision to protect past actions retrospectively. Most public enterprises were incorporated under the Company Act. Keeping the legal personality and the management intact, the assets and liabilities of one company were sold to other companies by the decision of the government, a process which was described as privatisation in Nepal. This act was challenged at the Supreme Court under public interest litigation by the same lawyer who had challenged the provisions of the Labour Act as ultra vires. Three more industries were privatised when the privatisation bill was in the process of obtaining royal assent. The drive for privatisation was so hasty that the government did not even bother to wait for the relevant legislation. At the time of writing, the Privatisation Act had not yet been enacted.

Nepal's experience of privatisation reminds us of Mahbub ul Haq's warning about seven sins. He was very realistic to warn against confused objectives, lack of transparency, concentration of assets, lack of competition, and a poor financial strategy. In the Nepali context, I am sure that many more than seven sins have already been committed.

An open door policy for foreign private investment is a top priority of the government. The objectives declared by the government are mainly as follows:

1. To build up a strong and dynamic economy by generating additional opportunities for income and employment through expanding productive activities;
2. To increase the participation of the private sector in the process of industrialisation;
3. To increase productivity by mobilising internal resources and materials in productive sectors and by importing foreign capital, modern technology management, and technical skills.
4. To increase the competitiveness of Nepali industries in international markets. Foreign investment is welcome in all sectors except defense industries which produce items like military armaments, ammunition or explosive materials, cigarettes, and alcohol.

To make foreign investment and the transfer of technology more attractive, the Foreign Investment and Transfer of Technology Act 1992 enables foreign private investments even in medium-size industries with less than NPR 20 million

(USD 170,534) in capital. Besides that, the act provides a rebate in taxes and the facility to repatriate profit. Similarly, the Industrial Enterprises Act 1992 guarantees against the nationalization of industries and other facilities. The most important change in the act is the one-window system in allowing an industry to work. About the work force, the act stipulates that a foreign worker can be employed for a maximum period of five years with the prior consent of the Department of Labour if an industry is unable to work without such manpower. Besides these changes, the government made very liberal declarations in order to attract foreign private investment to Nepal. Until now, however, there has been no substantial success because the most vital environment for industrial investment is still lacking in Nepal.

The government, with the help of the United Nations Industrial Development Organisation (UNIDO), organized the Nepal Investment Forum in 1992. A total of 306 businessmen from 26 countries participated. About 128 letters of intent for investments totalling about USD 740 million were signed. Investments from China topped the list, followed by those from India. Licenses have been issued to 230 joint venture and 100 per cent foreign investment industrial projects. Similar attempts were made in 1982 and 1984, too. But no substantial commitment has materialised. No further progress on the commitments made in 1992 has been made. The public has not been made aware of the relevant facts. No liberalisation of the law is going to attract big foreign private investment in Nepal until its hurdles with the market are solved. The main hurdle is uninterrupted access to the sea. No private investment, national or foreign, has come close to the size of grants from China and Russia over the past three decades. Nepal's close economic ties with India remained only as an extension of

India's domestic market. Mr. Bhattarai, after negotiating with India in June 1990, declared that India would become Nepal's market, reversing the past, which had made Nepal a reserved market of India. Despite his declaration, Nepal has remained a reserved market with an exceedingly large adverse balance of payments.

The lesson for Nepal is that until it has access to permanent, economical and convenient transit as a right, even the humblest plan for poverty alleviation or economic amelioration is impossible. This is a bitter truth which, unfortunately, is not always publicly discussed because of fear of annoying a big neighbour and the perception that it would be counterproductive. But there must be somebody, somewhere who can speak out about factual matters, pleading for a good cause with a neighbour. Though this is not a very appropriate forum to discuss bilateral problems, when we talk about the right to economic development as a nation, we cannot avoid such issues.

Poverty in Nepal is a double-faceted challenge as unemployment is increasing and economic growth, decreasing. Both problems are interlinked. The globalisation of the economy has not diminished the role of the nation-state. Instead, it has forced every nation to take care of its own economic problems. No nation can survive with a permanent hope for grant aid. The nation-state must have command over its economic activities. Small nations need to care more for their permanent sovereignty over their natural resources as well as the right to determine their economic activities as a matter of the right to self-determination. Threats of colonial domination and exploitation in different forms and manifestations still exist in several areas. Small and poor nations need great help and support to preserve their rights as nations. Developing countries have the "right to aid". In the regional context too, the "right to aid" has to be honoured by rich nations to bring up the level of economy of poor nations.

Nepal has received a great deal of aid from developed countries. Without it, the nation would have economically collapsed. Besides grants, preferential imports of woolen carpets in Germany and Switzerland and readymade garments in the United States are noticeable. Nepal cannot expect as much from India as it too is a developing country beset by various problems. However, in the matter of regulating immigrants and facilitating Nepal's access to the sea, India can extend more generous cooperation than it currently does. As far as other nations of the South Asia region are concerned, all are near to and surround India and need India's cooperation to come closer. The idea of mutual cooperation came very late but has had remarkable success. Countries of the region have come up with the Agreement on SAARC Preferential Trading Arrangement (SAPTA) to advance the mutual interests of SAARC member nations. This and many other steps are the best hope for the countries in the region. At present, all of Nepal's attempts, despite the enormous sympathy of the world community, have failed to achieve what Nepal desires as a nation. Without the economic independence to determine its economic activities, a nation cannot maintain its political independence. And, without the political independence of a nation, the freedoms and political liberties of persons cannot be exercised. The right to economic development is, in fact, included under the basic human rights of people. The independence of a nation cannot be measured in terms of the size of its economy. Like any nation, Nepal has to pay a price for its political as well as economic independence. No unjust and unequal conditions imposed upon it can alienate it from its rights as a nation and deny its citizens their rights. The law in Nepal is clear on this issue. The problem is Nepal's capability to implement its laws. The world is working collectively to achieve independence for all countries and freedom for all individuals. Now, on a regional basis, too, on the basis of sovereign equality, an equitable, just and viable order among countries has to be achieved. And this discussion should be maintained with an open and democratic spirit.

(Paper presented at the Third SAARC Law Conference)

III

B.P. Koirala: Philosopher, Statesman and Guide

A decade after he passed away, B.P. Koirala remains a towering philosopher, statesman and guide. Once he joined politics in Nepal, he captured and dominated its centre stage. The impact he created and bequeathed to the nation is both revolutionary as well as pacifistic. He was so forceful in his commitment that he led two rebellions; one succeeded and the other was aborted. Though at one time he resorted to violent revolution, he was, by temperament, humane and compassionate. His innocent, child-like smile was an asset to his personality. He always looked younger than he was, both in appearance as well as in spirit. He held various interpretations of youth. A person, according to him, is young as long as he is receptive to new ideas and capable of responding with vigour and enthusiasm. He was very sharp in logic and capable of rationalizing most of the complicated issues of his time.

Koirala led his Nepali Congress party to victory in the first free parliamentary election in 1959. He infused confidence in the people through his egalitarian declarations. At the international stage, he projected Nepal as a modern and democratic nation. He righted the wrong committed by Indian Prime Minister Jawaharlal Nehru in his interpretation of the Peace and Friendship Treaty between Nepal and India and obtained an apology from the Chinese Prime Minister Zhou Enlai over border skirmishes. Former Soviet Union leader Nikita Khrushchev gave him as much importance as he gave Dwight D. Eisenhower of the United States. Yet Koirala preferred to champion the cause of small and developing nations.

As a student of economics, I had several occasions to listen to his speeches. I found him very much aware of the economic laws of development. His role as the prime minister was not merely confined to executive functions. He emerged as a charismatic leader with complete dedication. India's leading journalist, Prem Bhatia, compared him to Nehru after observing him during the speech he gave in Tel Aviv.

Developments in Nepal took a mysterious turn in December 1960; Koirala was dismissed, imprisoned for eight years, and then spent the same number of years in self-exile in India. Under such circumstances, any person of ordinary mettle would have lost all energy and zeal to continue in politics. Koirala, in contrast, was always in search of an opportunity to start a dialogue for reconciliation even during the periods he was engaged in armed action against the regime.

Meanwhile, his expectation of Indian support for promoting the cause of democracy in Nepal began to fade. He had the courage to address an Indian audience and charge that India was being governed in the same old imperial pattern. He was not prepared to toe the line dictated to him. Koirala told an emissary of Indira Gandhi that he would rather remain a subject of his king than to serve India's interest.

He had an alert and active mind which could analyse political trends from a broad perspective. After the events following the bifurcation of Pakistan and the annexation of Sikkim by India, he saw the trend set by India's alliance with the Soviet Union. Soon after the termination of the Vietnam War, forces that led to the conflict of the Cold War had the possibility of concentrating in South Asia. He was actually prophetic in predicting that the whole of South Asia was going to be a zone of turmoil. In such a situation, the top priority for him in Nepal was nationalism. He saw a new patriotic responsibility to defend the independence of the country from foreign machinations. He decided to end his period of exile in India and return to Nepal, where he faced persecution and, possibly, capital punishment. He firmly declared that the struggle for democracy would become meaningless if the nation lost its existence.

This was a unique example of a leader of a state, after having taken up arms against the state, returning unarmed, without regret for his actions, and calling for national reconciliation. When he wanted to know my views before returning home, I told him that, with his return, he would be more revolutionary than Lenin and more pacifistic than Mahatma Gandhi. He was capable of adapting his political strategy to a changed circumstance. Lenin had no chance to prove his revolutionary courage by appearing unarmed to face persecution and Mahatma Gandhi had no charges against him to show his pacifistic courage. There were some who questioned Koirala's courage, asking him whether he had reached a secret understanding with, or an assurance from, the king. He said there was no such understanding or assurance, arguing that he relied upon his own analysis of the regional situation. It was his sincerity and courage of conviction which made him a legend in Nepali politics.

Koirala, known popularly as B.P., did with patriotic initiatives what he could not with arms. Soon after ending his exile in India in 1976 and returning to Nepal, panchayat politics also started moving. In the process of restructuring the polity, a referendum was held, and political reforms advanced. Inspite of the willingness of the king to accommodate all political interests, time did not allow him to proceed as he wished. A drastic change occurred in the country, for which the national reconciliation pronounced by B.P. did not get credit.

The concept of forging an alliance between nationalist and democratic forces according to the spirit of national reconciliation was dismissed by B.P.'s colleagues. They suspected that they would never come to power if they continued the policy of national reconciliation. Today, his Nepali Congress party is in power (1991–1994) and lots of tributes and homilies are paid in his memory. Institutes, academies and foundations are named after him. But his essential message has been lost. In his last public meetings, B.P. reminded the people of the strength and appeal of nationalism and emphasised that the tremendous potential of nationalism in Nepal was the best guarantee against its subjugation. He added that as long as his party followed a policy of national reconciliation, it would be a decisive force in the national politics. He warned that the party would be irrelevant the moment it ignored nationalism.

The country today is being governed under a political system other than the one championed by B.P. But the transition came in a way very different from what he had visualised. His views regarding nationalism and national interest seem to have been ignored by the people in power.

He was undeterred in his faith in the nationalist elements in the country. He used to complain that the members of his party were not convinced of the efficacy of the policy of national reconciliation. In anguish, he used to say, in his last days, that he would have proved its efficacy by bringing the party to power had he survived two years more. It took eight years for the party to come to power but only by changing its policy from reconciliation to confrontation and accepting external support.

In my view, B.P.'s colleagues, including his own brother, Girija Prasad Koirala, defied nationalistic trends by supporting India's economic blockade against Nepal in 1989 and by inviting Indian politicians to their party to threaten the king. These unpatriotic moves only alienated them from nationalist elements. The country today is under serious threat of instability, raising questions not only about the future of democracy but that about the nation's independence. The previous conflict between the partyless and multiparty system was understandable. What is not understandable is why the differences cannot be resolved within the framework of the democratic constitution. What B.P. had warned has turned out to be real: the forces of destabilization are indeed at work again. As it is located between two big regional powers—China and India—Nepal cannot afford to lean towards either of them. In order to build up resistance against pressure from either side, Nepal's leaders must hold fast to nationalism. This is where the policy of national reconciliation proves to be still relevant. Unfortunately, B.P.'s followers do not seem to have the purpose of the courage of conviction to call for national unity and nationalism. The best tribute to him would be to adhere to both nationalism and democracy.

(This commentary was first published in Spotlight newsmagazine, 23 July 1993)

IV

Nepal and India: A Crisis in Coexistence

Prime Minister Girija Prasad Koirala used to argue that Nepal-India relations would improve as soon as multiparty democracy was restored because the ties remained disturbed as a result of the conflicting political values espoused by the two countries. His endorsement of India's economic blockade against Nepal marked a reversal in the national reconciliation policy propounded by his noble brother, leader, and mentor B.P. Koirala, who had perceived a foreign design against Nepal's sovereignty and independence. Now that not only the multiparty system has been revived but also Koirala has come to power, he has the onus to prove that his statements were not uttered merely to bring him to power. Despite the changes, India's attitude remains rigid.

With a communist regime in the north and a democratic regime in the south, Koirala used to say human rights and democracy were the basic tenets of his foreign policy. It remains to be seen how the balance between the two will be maintained. However, Nepal finds it easier to condemn an authoritarian regime in remote Haiti than nearer home in Bhutan, which obviously is under the military protection of the world's largest democracy. Keeping national interest as its priority, India has the best relations with autocratic Bhutan but the worst with democratic Sri Lanka. Signals are not encouraging to Nepal's present government. Regardless of their values, Indian leaders share a broad consensus on foreign policy when it comes to their national interests. Koirala has a challenging task in New Delhi to make them realise Nepal's national interests.

In a speech made at the Red Fort in Delhi in the presence of Jawaharlal Nehru, B.P. Koirala had said that there could not be any irreconcilable conflict of interest between a nationalist Nepali and a nationalist Indian as long as ulterior designs did not pervert either. His younger brother will now have to prove whether or not that was correct.

Indian Prime Minister P.V. Narasimha Rao, who was the foreign minister during the 1989–90 blockade, is on record as having stated that he wanted to bring India-Nepal relations to the same ideal stage as when the 1950 Treaty was signed. He did not, however, eulogise the autocratic regime for having come to that understanding.

Is it possible to reverse Nepal-India ties back to 1950? There has been a sea change since then as, with the advent of democracy in 1951, Nepal ended its period of isolation and began to rapidly expand its political and economic ties with the outside world. Nepal, along with India, was one of the founding members of the non-aligned movement. It plays a prominent role in the United Nations and other world bodies. Because of a common commitment to non-alignment and respect for each other's sovereign equality, several unjust provisions of the treaty had already become irrelevant, but these were not adopted in the law. The treaty's provision for mutual consultation at the moment of foreign aggression also became irrelevant due to subsequent developments. Nepal entered into a peace and friendship treaty with China. India fought wars with China and Pakistan; Nepal, which was never consulted, maintained neutrality. India acquiesced to the new relationship between the two countries. The Nepali Army played a role in international peacekeeping missions on several occasions. The Zone of Peace proposal made in 1975 has won the support of 116 countries. The situation is thus vastly different than what it was in 1950.

There have been major changes in the region, too. China has emerged as a military power to the north of Nepal. Pakistan's bifurcation gave birth to a new nation—Bangladesh. Sikkimese fighting against their monarch lost their independent national identity. To strengthen its security, India entered into a virtual military alliance with the Soviet Union in 1971, heightening fear and insecurity in the countries of the region. This forced these countries to seek protection elsewhere. Soviet military interference in Afghanistan brought the USSR closer to South Asian affairs. India's support for terrorism and later its fight against it reveals India's crisis in the region. The decline of Soviet military power has forced India to rethink its relations with its neighbours. Without the backing of the Soviet army, India has an opportunity to take the initiative in establishing peaceful co-existence with its neighbours. India needs particularly to show its concern for the nationalist sentiments of small neighbours, sentiments which have been the drive of modern times. Amidst these developments, Nepal-India ties have required new elements which cannot be eliminated. Regressing to the stage of 1950 would be virtually impossible.

The 1950 treaty did not come under serious debate until a controversy was sparked following a brief skirmish between Nepali and Chinese border troops in 1960, when B.P. Koirala was the prime minister. Nehru came out with a statement claiming that the security of Nepal was India's responsibility, a statement assertively contradicted by Koirala. Contradicting what Nehru had said, Koirala emphasised: "Nepal was a fully sovereign and independent nation which decides its external and home policy according to its own judgement and its own liking without ever referring to any outside authorities." Nehru then admitted that "Koirala's interpretation of the Treaty was completely correct and he had correctly interpreted the Treaty." Perhaps, there was a meeting of the minds of the two statesmen, who both genuinely wanted the conflict to subside in their respective national interests.

During the panchayat regime, India blew hot and cold. Nepal's modernisation created needs that strained bilateral relations. India's desire to discipline Nepal like Bhutan, if not Sikkim, always created friction between the two countries. In pursuance of that strategy, the India-imposed economic blockade was one measure which Nepal, with world opinion in her favour, survived. India, backed by her allies, tried to use the movement for democracy in Nepal to negotiate the best bargain with harassed panchayat leaders in the same way it had done in 1950 with the autocratic regime. But it was a different Nepal in 1990.

Revival of democracy did not end the controversy regarding the interpretation of the treaty. Instead of promptly signing fresh treaties of trade and transit as Nepalis had expected, India agreed to restore the status quo ante as of April 1987 (not March 1989, when the treaties were terminated). This makes it obvious that it does not matter to the government of India what form of government and what rulers rule Nepal. Finding Nepal roiling in internal conflict when the movement was in full swing and its leaders were jailed, an Indian delegation visited Kathmandu with a draft treaty which even Bhutan would have refused to sign. There are indications that the same draft has persisted despite the revival of democracy.

It is intriguing that attempts to destabilise even a multiparty regime have continued unabated. People like Ram Raja Prasad Singh have found much space in India's prominent dailies to declare armed insurrection against the present regime, too. Quixotic Subhas Ghising's "Greater Nepal" bogey is nothing but a hate campaign against Nepal and Nepalis, one which has found a very favourable place in India, though the Indian people cannot imagine Nepal ever swallowing India. It is a well-known fact that the press in India toe the government policy line as far as foreign affairs are concerned. What would be India's reaction if some elements in India chose to propagate insurrection against and disintegration against it from Nepal?

In a cryptic statement in parliament, Koirala said the treaties of 1950 and 1965 would be reviewed but did not elaborate. He was either wrongly briefed or deliberately failed to mention the annulled agreement for the procurement of arms and training from India in 1965. The agreement was good for neither country. In addition, it provoked China. Following the agreement, ties with China worsened, as was reflected in a publicly issued condemnation of "American imperialists, Soviet revisionists, Indian expansionists and Nepali reactionaries" and that they would "break their skulls in the streets of Kathmandu." This Chinese reaction, perhaps, resulted in the abrogation of the agreement in 1969. The grave lesson is again that, as a yam between two boulders, Nepal could not lean militarily to either side. Any attempt to review the agreement in disguise would gravely endanger regional peace.

In order to woo the other side, politicians speak of a special relation without explaining which side would bear the greater burden. The price for the special relation has always been very heavy on Nepal.

To improve relations, the country now needs a long term, if not a permanent, transit treaty in accordance with international law. If the 1950 Peace and Friendship Treaty, which is of less importance, is valid for an indefinite period, why does the transit right need periodical renewal? Nepal's transit right was restricted and rendered ineffective by combining it with the agreement "Cooperation to Control Unauthorised Trade."

The future of Nepal's economy depends on harnessing water resources, an activity which is partly technical and partly financial. The concept of a common river is detrimental to Nepal's interests. Trade between the two countries must be on the basis of mutual benefit, a criterion which, over the last few decades, Nepal has built up its confidence to demand. The MFN regime has contributed some positive experiences for trade diversification.

Another important issue is immigration. With a population of less than 20 million, Nepal cannot be expected to offer job opportunities to India's population of 1 billion. Reciprocity in this matter would eliminate Nepal's identity and Nepalis would find themselves a minority in their own nation. The migration of Nepal's entire population to India, in contrast, would still constitute an insignificant minority.

These are the areas where Nepal's interests have to be properly safeguarded in order to have a lasting relation. Indian leaders have to accept the fact that their democracy cannot afford a colonial deal with its small neighbour.

The end of World War II unleashed an upsurge in cries for national independence. The independence of India and the liberation of China were its immediate results. The culmination of the situation forced a change in Nepal, too, in 1951. Again, there has been an upsurge in nationalism in Eastern Europe and the Soviet Union. Mass uprisings in Eastern Europe were directed more against foreign-imposed regimes than their own authoritarian rule. Similarly, drastic changes in favour of democracy could not hold republics within the Soviet Union; all followed the Baltic example. The Czarist empire which had become the Soviet Union could not suppress the power of nationalism for long.

Nepal, which has a long habit of living independently as a sovereign nation, expects respect for its nationalist sensitivities. India has to enlarge its heart a little bit in proportion to its size to ensure peaceful co-existence with neighbouring Nepal.

Once I asked a Nepali octogenarian politician who had the privilege of intimacy with almost all prime ministers of independent India how those ministers wanted to see Nepal. He told me he was utterly ignorant about what they wanted in Nepal. The confusion persists.

(The commentary was first published in
The Independent Weekly, 6 November 1991)

V

Problems in the Electoral System in Nepal

Of what efficacy are rules of procedure in securing the end of justice if the moral condition of the people is such that witnesses generally lie and judges and their subordinates take bribes? Again, how can institutions provide good municipal administration if there exists such indifference to the subject that those who would administer honestly and capably cannot be induced to serve and the duties are left to those who undertake them because they have some private interest to be promoted? Of what avail is the most broadly popular representative system if the electors do not care to choose the best member of parliament but choose the individual who spends the most money to be elected? How can a representative assembly work for good if its members can be bought or their excitability of temperament, uncorrected by public discipline or private self-control, makes them incapable of calm deliberation and they resort to manual violence on the floor of the House or shoot at one another with rifles? How, again, can the government, or any other joint concern, be carried on in a tolerable

> manner by people so envious that if one among them seems likely to succeed in anything, those who ought to co-operate with him form a tacit combination to make him fail? Whenever the general disposition of the people is such that each individual regards those only of his interests which are selfish and does not dwell on, or concern himself for, his share of general interest, in such a state of things good government is impossible.
>
> – John Stuart Mill
> *Considerations on Representative Government*

After a trial with partyless democracy for about three decades, the 1990 Constitution of the Kingdom of Nepal restored multiparty parliamentary democracy under a constitutional monarchy. In a drastic departure from the past, this constitution was promulgated by King Birendra on the assertive advice and consent of the Council of Ministers, which had legal authority under the Constitution of 1962. Before being abrogated, the previous constitution legitimised a public upheaval against the political system under it. The 1990 Constitution is, in fact, the outcome of a national consensus of a very extraordinary nature in a period of unusual turmoil in the country.

In its search for an appropriate form of government, Nepal has undergone momentous changes in the past. Every such change has forced a new shape in the constitution. Having a very long and complex history of constitutional law, Nepal started the practice of having a formal written constitution in 1948. The first constitution was the Government of Nepal Act 1948. It became irrelevant after the revolution in 1951. This was repealed by the Interim Government of Nepal Act 1951 as this was an interim arrangement. The Constitution of the Kingdom of Nepal promulgated in 1958 was drafted along the Westminster model with the expert opinion of Sir Ivor

Jennings. It established not only a pluralist parliamentary system of governance but also the partyless panchayat system under its emergency provisions. The draft was so compact in form that the pluralist parliamentary system could not be completely overthrown as long as that constitution survived. But this, the most democratic constitution Nepal had, prolonged an emergency period beyond the norm. It was ultimately abrogated by the Constitution of 1962.

The Constitution of 1962, which introduced a partyless democracy, lasted for a long time. It had three major amendments and survived a national referendum on the form of government. The 1962 Constitution, the fifth written constitution in practice, had all the ingredients of the democratic development of the constitution. The form of government under the constitution is popular as well as representative. The executive power of the state was made responsible to the parliament and parliamentary legislation was subject to judicial review. Serving as a watchdog over functionaries of the authorities of the state is an ombudsman-like body in the constitution. Besides, the Public Service Commission and the Controller-General to guard the fairness and accountability of the government, the constitution created a powerful Election Commission to hold periodic elections to the Parliament and local governments. The Election Commission conducted two general elections and two by-elections for the House of Representatives and two periodical elections for the Rashtriya Sabha, the Upper-House of the Parliament. Similarly, the Election Commission held one general election for about four thousand villages and thirty-six town units of the local government.

The experience of the past has become a matter of history. The 1990 Constitution is fresh in the test. Any debate over the efficacy of the form of government and method of representation is too premature to be launched. The ideas and institutions introduced by any constitution have to be made adequately familiar to and temperamentally accepted by long practice and obedience by the people. It takes a long time to build up traditions and conventions to give support to the functioning of the constitution. A constitution promulgated after a period of political instability needs great national consensus to get a root in the society. Constitutionalism promotes the rule of law and pacifies a tendency for upheavals and revolutions. Once a society is destabilised in such a way, even if the best of constitutions is promulgated, it takes a long time to stabilise its structures. A successful model of the constitution of one social condition may not bring the same result in another social situation. This fact was proved by the failure of the British model of constitution recommended by a great authority of constitution, Sir Ivor Jennings, in Nepal in 1958. It has been proved by Nepal's experiences that differences in social conditions and political traditions bring different results even under the same model of constitution.

Nepal has some unique features of political development. The form of government and other political institutions which are the product of the post-industrial revolution in the West were not very strange in countries with a colonial background. Free from such a colonial legacy, the growth of institutions and habits and attitudes in the matter of governance have followed a different pattern in Nepal. It has no model of similar background on the way to modernisation. Linking the two very big geographical units of Central and South Asia, Nepal has a long record of peace with stability and change with continuity. In its own way, it was able to preserve its national independence and sovereign status, but it lagged very much behind in the process of modernisation, development and democracy. With a multi-ethnic, multi-racial and multi-lingual composition, Nepal has the social and cultural roots it needs for pluralism. Despite having its own independent and indigenous political development, Nepal has a lot to learn and improve from the experience of others in the region and beyond.

The 1990 Constitution declares that the people are sovereign. Consistent with that, every adult above the age of 18 has a right to exercise the franchise in the elections for the House of Representatives as well as for local government units. Because of the multiparty objectives of the constitution, the role of political parties in the matter of the representation of the people is very specific. Everybody has the right to organise a political party. The constitution is very explicitly in favour of a multiparty state and is against the concept of a one-ideology state. This can be seen in many provisions of the constitution. A multiparty system is one of the unamendable basic features of the constitution. Political parties have become unavoidable in the structure of power. The king nominates a leader of the political party that commands a majority in the House of Representatives as the prime minister. In case no political party has a majority in the House, a person who commands the support of two or more parties is nominated as the prime minister. If that kind of coalition is not possible, the king nominates the leader of the largest political party in the House of Representatives as the prime minister. On the recognition of a political party for the purpose of elections, the constitution fixes a minimum number of popular votes received in the election. Some recent cases decided by the Supreme Court addressed this provision. In the writ petition filed by Prasant Maharjan, a Special Bench of the Supreme Court declared:

"Multiparty system has been accepted as the basic feature of the constitution and Article 116 has been made unamendable. It has been restricted to enact or arrange any law in contravention to that provision of the constitution. The interpretation or the use of the constitution has to be done in accordance with the main provision of the constitution."

The petitioner in the case unsuccessfully challenged the condition imposed by the Election Commission regarding the minimum votes procured by a political party as stipulated by the constitution.

In one case, the majority of the Special Bench again declared that the condition for a national-level party required for the purpose of an election was a valid order. The Supreme Court, in response to a petition filed by Prabhu Narayan Choudhary, said that the condition worked against the extreme proliferation of political parties in the election: "By the restrictive provision of Article 113 (2), it may seem against democratic concepts. But the architects of the constitution clearly appeared to have taken in view the background of the political history of the country. Democratic practice and culture are not much developed and refined in Nepal. Some restrictions appeared to have been considered necessary for the consolidation of the multiparty system in the infancy period of democracy." The Supreme Court, in that case, reiterated that the multiparty system is an unamendable basic structure of the constitution. It also explained the role visualised in the constitution regarding the articulation of interests and popular representation by competitive political parties.

The constitution has, thus, made provisions for various democratic institutions and provided opportunities to citizens for a good government as well as self-government, both of which are considered to be supreme objectives in any democracy. But democracy is not a legal document only. Human factors are essential to give shape to democracy and make it materialise. Democracy remains an abstract idea if institutions fail to deliver the expected results and human elements act contrary to their desired roles. A change becomes irrelevant if the attitudes, temperaments and habits of the people concerned remain unchanged. A constitution stands on a human assumption regarding its enforceability. It declares the popular will as supreme, but that does not automatically arouse such will in the people. For the growth and development of democratic institutions and formation of democratic habits and culture, a great deal of patience and tolerance is needed. A legal instrument can hardly ensure such a change.

Nepal has not yet gone past the first phase of its contract with democracy. Its experience with democratic institutions and ideas is limited to within this formative period. Perversions have not yet become acute, but Nepal is not far away from that menace. A timely precaution within the constitution can help ensure the fair representation of the people in the governance of the nation. Reviewing the past performances and problems, the following issues need to be considered seriously:

1. Method of election
2. Instrumentalities of conducting elections
3. Identification of voters
4. Effective control and supervision by constitutional authorities
5. Control over irregular expenses
6. Democratisation of political parties
7. Public vigilance

1. Method of Election

Elections are held for the Parliament and local government units differently. The method of election for the Rashtriya Sabha, the Upper House, is mainly indirect and based on the system of proportional representation. The 60-member Rashtriya Sabha, or National Assembly, consists of 35 members, including at least three women members, elected by the Pratinidhi Sabha, the Lower House, or House of Representatives, on the basis of proportional representation by means of a single transferable vote. Another 15 members, three from each of the five development regions, are elected on the basis of a single transferable vote by an elected college consisting of the chiefs and deputy chiefs of village- and town-level authorities, and the chiefs, deputy chiefs and other district-level authorities. Ten members are nominated by the king from among persons who have made prominent contributions to various fields of national life. The Pratinidhi Sabha is elected from single-member constituencies using a first-past-the-post system of election.

After the experience of the unicameral legislature of the panchayat period, Nepal's 1990 Constitution instead provides for two houses in the parliament. As the role of the Upper House is to compel rethinking rather than to reject, its members represent diverse sections of the society. If persons of outstanding calibre are nominated for the position, the utility of the Upper House can be assessed properly. Till now, however, most positions have been awarded on unknown considerations and, therefore, the role of such persons also goes unnoticed by people in general. The constitution had a clear purpose in creating the Upper House but that purpose is not properly understood by the people who make decisions about such nominations.

The most important role in Parliament is that of the 205-member Pratinidhi Sabha. This house is elected on the basis of the largest number of votes in the respective constituencies. At the time of the drafting of the constitution, there was a debate about whether Nepal should adopt a proportional representation system or a first-past-the-post system of election. There was a consensus in favour of the first-past-the-post system mainly on the consideration of the stability provided by a strong government. The constitution made a multiparty system one of its basic structures, but it does not desire an extreme multiplicity of political parties.

Of the 42 political parties registered in the Election Commission in 1991, only seven were able to acquire the requisite three per cent of total votes polled to maintain their symbols for the next election. There were 24 political parties in the election of 1994, but only four were able to preserve their symbols. There is a tendency for the emergence of a two-party system partly because of the first-past-the-post system of election and partly because of the political polarisation of the Nepali Congress (NC) party and the Communist Party of Nepal-Unified Marxist Leninist (UML). Out of the total votes polled in 1991, the NC secured 39.50 percent and the UML got 29.97 percent. Because there were a large number of parties in the contest in 1991, votes were split into many camps and, therefore, the result was that the government having a majority in the house had, in fact, represented a minority of less than 40 per cent of the votes cast. In the second general election in 1994, out of the total votes polled, the NC secured 33.38 percent, which was the highest but much less than in the previous election and the UML received 30.85 percent, slightly more than in the previous election. (A survey found that the

NC was in second position in 95 constituencies, followed by the UML in 56 constituencies).

These facts indicate that the election system ensures a popular government and not a representative one. As there was no political party to claim a majority, the UML formed a minority government as it was the largest party in the House of Representatives. The first-past-the-post system ensures a popular government but not one that is fully representative. It does not fulfill its objectives when a large number of parties and independent candidates divide votes among themselves. Even when parties are not viable in terms of their being able to serve as an alternative power, some parties persist in participating in elections and causing the threat of a hung parliament. It would be considered a failure of this election system if a government having command over less than one-third of the votes cast aspired to complete the full term of Parliament.

Realising the anomaly, the UML, unlearning the Communist dogma of class struggle, elicited support from all for its government-by-consensus in 1994–95. It would be very interesting to see their strategy become successful at this stage of political development. Even if the possibility of another general election appears imminent, the nation is not in the mood to switch over to another more representative system of election. Under the last two constitutions, several methods of elections were experimented with, and the people found this latest system more practical than the earlier ones.

2. Instrumentalities of Conducting Elections

The constitution has created a very powerful Election Commission, provided it assumes its full responsibility. The chief election commissioner and other commissioners are appointed by the king on the recommendation of the Constitutional Council. The purpose of the Constitutional Council is to keep those positions free from the fear and favour of the executive and give them popular sanction too. The tenure of the post is five years. The most significant condition in the service regards the restriction on appointment to any government service after retirement. But the spirit of this condition has not been respected in practice. The first chief election commissioner, after completing the election to the first parliament and local government units, resigned from his post without providing any reasonable grounds for his resignation, and, soon after that, he was appointed as the ambassador to the United Kingdom by the king upon the recommendation of the prime minister. This has set a trend that a prime minister can "pick up" an unwanted commissioner even though the constitution does not allow the "kicking out" of that person. Such apprehensions in the minds of the people affect the public faith in institutions. No constitution can elaborate a code of conduct to such a high repository of power. One has to read the spirit of the constitution between the lines. To generate real faith in the constitution, the basic law of the land has to be respected, not only in letter but in spirit, too. But in the game of power, persons in power ignore such lessons of history.

Since the panchayat days, to establish credibility in elections, judges of lower courts have been appointed as returning officers to conduct elections. This tradition of involving the judiciary in administrative action has been maintained with much inconvenience to the litigant public. The 1990 Constitution vaguely authorised the deputation of judges of the district and appeal courts for election activities after consultation with the Judicial Council. In the performance of that duty, these judges have to remain under the executive discipline of the Election Commission, a position which is not congenial to their judicial role. Without amending the law, judges could be relieved of this onerous task. However, the big gap in credibility between the general administration and the public has forced the Election Commission to involve judicial cadres in this difficult job.

Nepal's bureaucracy has always been a target of vendettas by successive governments. Changes in the political system have not greatly changed the practice of using the bureaucracy arbitrarily. The result is the loss of the image and credibility of the bureaucracy. The law, however, has sufficient safeguards for the service, and, for the first time, the Supreme Court provided a remedy to a large number of victimised civil servants. If one considers this judiciously, one realises there is enough scope to protect and enhance the morale of the civil service. A large number of senior civil servants were compulsorily retired by the previous government without any grounds, a practice which the Supreme Court has now declared arbitrary and nullified. Since this decision, the government has, for the first time, realised the limits of its power against the bureaucracy. Unless attitudes are changed, the bureaucracy of the country will not be able to command the trust of the people in conducting free and fair elections. All major parties need to reach a consensus to hold elections with the help of administrative cadres and keep the judiciary active in its own area.

3. Identification of Voters

Every citizen who is above 18 years of age has a general right to vote and has a duty under the law to get his name added to the voters' list as soon as he or she is óf age. It is a legal obligation on the part of the Election Commission, too, to update the voters' list at the end of each year. There are adequate provisions in the law for keeping the record exact and up-to-date. But such updating has never been done. A substantial percentage of qualified citizens cannot find their names on the voters' list. The biggest problem has been voting by assuming a false personality, a practice which is also known as proxy voting. There is an all-party consensus to tackle this problem of impersonation.

In the 1994 winter session of Parliament, the House of Representatives unanimously passed a resolution to introduce identity cards for each voter for the next election. But after the drama of a mid-term dissolution of the House in June 1995, it was unfeasible to implement that resolution. The Election Commission declared that it would conduct the next by-election in three constituencies which had been vacated by winners of two seats each by distributing identity cards to voters. To that end, it forwarded a draft of the statute to the government. As there has been no prompt move on the side of the government to bring the necessary legislation, there may arise a conflict between the Election Commission and the government. The party in power has an obligation in this respect to fulfil its promise to implement the resolution of the parliament. The cost of issuing identity cards is much less than holding another mid-term general election without any convincing grounds for doing so.

4. *Effective Control and Supervision by Constitutional Authorities*

The law in Nepal provides adequate safeguards and remedies against all abuses and excesses of power, too. The problem here is not the lack of laws, but the lack of implementation of those laws and the inaction of authorities. As a last resort or remedy, the Supreme Court has been exercising its extraordinary powers to a great extent. As other institutions have not been able to imbibe the progressive concepts of law adopted by the court, it has become difficult to generate faith in there being an effective remedy available in the constitution among most people. Hence, extremism has gained ground. The Supreme Court has decided a large number of cases according to the authority of the previous constitution. On many occasions, the court had to confront executive authorities and bear the brunt of their actions. The Supreme Court is still under great strain to maintain its effective role under the present constitution. The constitution has suddenly aroused very high expectations from the judiciary, and especially from the Supreme Court. The time is not yet ripe to evaluate its performance in the changed context.

The 1990 Constitution generated great hope from the Commission for the Investigation of Abuse of Authorities (CIAA), which is perhaps more powerful than the ombudsman in constitutional terms. It has the power to investigate and make enquiries about any person holding any public office. In addition, it can even prosecute people in the court for charges framed by it. In an ordinary situation, the attorney general has the right to make a final decision about whether to initiate proceedings in any case on behalf of His Majesty's Government in any court or before a judicial authority. The most important thing the CIAA has to do is to submit annual reports to His

Majesty on the works it has performed. Those reports are ultimately presented before the parliament, a measure which helps the government remain open and transparent.

However, the results have never been in the spirit of the constitution. A large number of complaints against people holding public offices come to the public's knowledge, but people rarely hear of any effective investigation being taken up by the CIAA. Complaints against people exercising state power become especially serious, and frustrating, at the time of elections. The problems during the panchayat system were very acute though there was a similar commission to investigate, prosecute and decide on the abuse of power under that system as well. At the time of elections, politicians demand a coalition government by all parties with a view to share the obvious advantages of power. During the panchayat period, a candidate backed by the government could enjoy all the facilities of the state to aid his or her win. The use of government vehicles and distribution of money and materials to influence voters were common practices which served only to degrade the standard of public behaviour.

The problem of such misuse of power and corruption is much worse at present. In the 1994 parliamentary election, the Election Commission issued some public statements regarding the misuse of government vehicles by a candidate who was a minister at the time. It issued a directive to the government asking it not to transfer government officials at the time of an election. These actions taken by the Election Commission had a positive impact upon the government though they were too little and too late to control the mischief. Within a given situation of law, the CIAA can play a great role in preventing abuse of power by public authorities. A free and fair election is not an isolated act in a democracy. It has to garner all-around institutional support. Unfortunately, such support is lacking in Nepal. An election has to be carried out through the concerted action of all the institutions of a state.

5. Control over Irregular Expenses

Everybody in Nepal is worried about the alarmingly high cost of election propaganda, a burden which, ultimately, the people have to bear. The previous government allocated an estimated amount of NPR 330 million but its actual expenses reached double that figure. If the expenses of all the prominent parties are taken into consideration, they seem to have spent almost the same amount of money. In some prestigious constituencies, candidates are believed to have spent about NPR 10 million each. The law in Nepal has fixed an upper limit of expenses by a candidate, but there is no precedent for penalizing a candidate for violating it despite the fact that its violation is a common occurrence. The Election Commission can impose a fine of up to NPR 5,000 if a candidate does not submit the details of his or her election expenses. This kind of provision has been in the statute book since the early days of panchayat, but there has never been any body to enforce it. If the Election Commission realised its obligation to enquire about the details of expenses, people could censure defaulters.

The high cost of election propaganda has increased corruption in public affairs. It is beyond the capacity of ordinary people to finance parties in an election. Even people in fair-sized industries and businesses cannot provide as large a sum of money to contesting candidates as they do in response to a serious natural calamity. Political parties rarely keep bank accounts. In a strategically important small country, it is a matter of serious worry that elections are held with the free play of suspicious financing.

6. Democratisation of Political Parties

In the democratisation of the country, some prominent political parties have played a historic role. Even when advocating in favour of the party system was a criminal offence in the country, a large number of people suffered prosecution in order to uphold their faith. But even these people have not been able to democratise their relations within the party. It is a matter of degree only, but no party has yet been able to allow delegates of the party to choose their programmes or leadership in a democratic way. Communist parties claim democratic centralism has worked, a claim which is very difficult to verify because their proceedings are closed. Almost all other parties with democratic declarations have personality-based leaderships in which some persons commit the same acts of indiscipline but continue in leadership while others are expelled using the excuse of maintaining discipline. Parties in the formative period are genuinely afraid of subverters and infiltrators. The fall of the government of the NC in 1994 was alleged to have been the result of internal subversion. This kind of apprehension has forced even persons of high integrity to act conspiratorially in order to promote personal interests at the cost of party interests. It is difficult to manage a democratic election when leaders of parties espouse a narrow view focused on promoting their own interests at the cost of all democratic norms and values.

7. Public Vigilance

The will of the people is a supreme force in a democracy. But this force has to be properly organised and activated. Elections are an occasion on which the people element gets maximum attention. Contesting parties use all the means in their reach to influence and win over the trust and support of the common people. During an election, a few alert and vigilant persons can create an opinion about the standard of that election internally as well as externally. Persons of outstanding calibre and reputation have been very successful in guarding against malpractice and high-handedness in elections. Since the 1991 parliamentary election, a team of national and international observers has watched and monitored the process of elections in most SAARC countries. Governments in this region particularly fear international opinion because of their increasing dependence on foreign aid and support.

International press and media also have a great influence on maintaining a minimum standard of fairness in elections. Whether it was the election conducted by Ferdinand Marcos in the Philippines or that conducted by another ruler in another country, if there was rampant irregularity in the election, it was always the international media which helped the people of the concerned country to undo that. In a fragile democracy in a developing country, these kinds of observation teams have been able to deter governments from rigging elections in favour of the ruling party and, at the same time, mitigate extremist and populist propaganda organised against a comparatively fair election. Nepal also had this kind of experience when opposition parties threatened mass agitations against the results of the 1991 parliamentary election. The impartial opinions of independent observers helped people to accept the results. One of the greatest sanctions within the capacity of the common people is the sanction of public opinion. The people must always be alert and vigilant and ready to exercise this sanction if there is to be a fair and free election.

In conclusion, elections are, in the real sense, an exercise of sovereign power by the people. In an election, people choose their representatives in parliament to run a government democratically and with their mandate. The ability and wisdom of the people determine the quality of a democratic government. All instruments of the state are justifiably supposed to provide a free and fair atmosphere in the exercise of this power. To maintain all these conditions, an alert and active citizenry is highly desirable. Because of the rampant ignorance and poverty of the people of developing countries, a class of elites is often able to grow its own vested interest in power, which it wants to grab by any means, making the people helpless choosers. One of the greatest preachers of non-violence, Mahatma Gandhi, used very harsh words against parliament, long before India became independent. Continuing where the Mahatma had left off, Jayaprakash Narayan added his anguish over a trend to reduce democracy "to mere casting of votes."

Despite such criticism, India has seen democracy operate continuously since its independence, continuity which is rare in developing countries. But, to a serious analyst, India's future seems to be very pessimistic. What Atul Kohli said about India in his book *Democracy and Discontentment* may very soon be the case in other countries, including Nepal. He said:

> India is still, of course, a functioning democracy, but increasingly it is not well governed. The evidence of eroding political order is everywhere. Personal rule has become

> party rule at all levels—national, and district. Below the rulers, the entrenched civil and police services have been politicized. Various social groups have pressed new and ever more diverse political demands in demonstration that often has led to violence. The omnipotent but feeble state, in turn, has vacillated; its responses have varied over a wide range: indifference, sporadic concessions, and repression, moreover have highlighted the breakdown of the civil machinery intended to enforce the law and maintain order. In order to protect themselves, citizens in some parts of the country have begun organizing private armies. The growing political violence has periodically brought the armed forces into India's political arena, whereas the armed forces once were considered apolitical.

Kohli went on to suggest a solution applicable to other democratic developing countries which is relevant to the present discussion:

> The concept of governability draws attention to the tasks a government can be expected to perform. For a democratic developing country like India, governability has been defined here as the capacity of rulers to do three things: maintain coalition support, initiate solution to problems perceived to be important, and resolve political conflicts without force and violence. Thus, a democratic developing country is well governed if its government can simultaneously sustain legitimacy, promote socioeconomic development, and maintain order without coercion. The growing incapacity in India to perform these tasks is what has been conceptualized in this study as a manifestation of a crisis of governability.

Nepal's problems are also related to non-governance. In mostly traditional socio-political conditions, Nepal has introduced modern ideas and instruments of governance. There is an obvious gap between the setting of ideals and the insurmountable realities. Nepal has enough experiments in reforms. The most essential reform now needed is in the attitude of the people concerned across the whole spectrum of politics. Gunnar Myrdal remarked that "development is an attitudinal factor." Our experience suggests that democracy, too, is an attitudinal factor. Merely adding a few more laws in the name of reform is definitely not going to reform the problem in representation.

VI

The Democratic World's Cause in Nepal

Prelude

Those watching Nepal before and after 1990 know the people of third-world countries. The overall mood of consensus, a very typical Nepali characteristic, existing among the three Nepali P's—people, parties and palace—contributed greatly to the young democracy's progress. But also, Nepal has problems when it comes to practicing democracy in the context of adverse, hard facts: poverty, illiteracy, the geopolitical interests of giant neighbours and, lastly, the priority lists of party elites exhausting themselves in power games.

Mr. Ganesh Raj Sharma, an eminent constitutional lawyer of Nepal, has kindly contributed to our NAMASKAR the following article reflecting his thoughts on and analysis of where Nepal stands today and where it could go tomorrow. He also suggests what could be done by the democratic world to promote the stabilisation of democracy in Nepal.

Mr. Sharma was a very intimate counsellor of late B.P. Koirala who, for his last accomplishment, was exploring the build-up of national consensus and reconciliation, both of which suffered after the death of Koirala.

The bold and highly intellectual views of Mr. Sharma are hailed by his friends and foes alike. With distance from power as well as populism, Mr. Sharma has a long record of defending cases of constitutional and democratic rights as well as those related to national interests. Among the ex-clients of Mr. Sharma are many political prisoners of the early, feared days of the panchayat, many of whom are today party elites, inside as well as people outside the current power in Nepal. The successful challenge to the Nepali government over the Tanakpur issue was his most famous recent case in the Supreme Court.

Madhav Raj Acharya, 22 November 1993

Multiparty democracy was revived in Nepal, a country strategically located between two emerging world powers—India and China—at a time when the disciplinarian panchayat polity could not withstand the pressure unleashed by India's economic blockade with a strategic purpose against it. That was a momentous time, a time when the Soviet political empire was crumbling and a wave of democracy swept all around the world. The people of Nepal rejoiced in a new form of constitutional monarchy. The purpose of the economic blockade—to promote India's strategy—remained unfulfilled.

But soon after assuming the executive responsibility, the prime minister moaned in crisis that "it was extremely difficult to run the government in a poor country." It was easy to bring people to the streets for violent agitation, but it was extremely difficult to mobilise a conscious and organised citizenry in a democratic manner. People are either persuaded or forced to barter their franchise for petty interests. As a result, not the people themselves but extraneous forces and financiers are emerging as major decision-makers in Nepali politics.

The root cause of this evil is definitely abject poverty and rampant illiteracy. Per capita income is less than USD 170 a year. Unemployment is growing. The majority of people in rural areas live below the subsistence level. Urbanisation has created slums. Modernisation has brought a "revolution of rising expectations." In such complex circumstances, democracy has to be meaningful to the people of Nepal.

The ruling party, once committed to democratic socialism, is reorienting its followers to a free-market economy and privatisation. Employment for the people is no longer considered the obligation of the government. Opportunities for higher education and training within the country are scarce. The fortunate few who have been educated and trained in other countries do not see any prospects in staying in the country. The government has followed the old tradition of purging officials from jobs; more than 7,000 civil servants were forced into retirement.

This decision has been challenged in the Supreme Court, with the argument that it was not only a gross violation of the rule of law but also a humiliation of public servants. Many of the dismissed officers have remained passive, however, because they consider it as irremediable tradition.

Western democracies have been paying a great deal of attention to the promotion of democracy in Nepal. Without such support, Nepal's democracy would have died prematurely. But a great deal more remains to be done. Unless this task gets priority, the prospects of democracy and social order in Nepal look rather feeble.

Politicians in power had unrealistic expectations from their democratic neighbour India as they had received encouragement against the previous regime. Now they are sad to see India hobnobbing with forces of destabilisation. There has not been any significant contribution from India to stabilise the democratic process in Nepal. For instance, Nepal faces a very serious influx of refugees, most of whom are from Bhutan, coming across the Indian border. Under a treaty with Bhutan, India has an obligation to treat the Bhutanese as nationals. Instead of fulfilling that obligation, however, India has forced the refugees into Nepal. Humanitarian assistance has flowed to Nepal from countries all over the world except India. Nepali leaders are in communication with Bhutan on the issue but no substantial gains have been made. Again, under a treaty with India, Bhutan has to be guided by India on foreign and defense matters. But when it comes to Bhutanese refugees, India has refused to undertake any such responsibility.

Landlocked Nepal remains handicapped in its efforts to achieve economic development. The British regime in India conceded a permanent right of transit to Nepal. This right was observed even many years after its India's independence. Now, however, Nepal has to negotiate a transit treaty every five years. Nepal's having to engage in periodic discussions of transit does not encourage long-term foreign investment in Nepal. Trade in commodities such as carpets and garments, which are exported via air cargo, is booming. Without an air link, Nepal would have neither foreign trade nor tourism. Losses in land transit are exorbitant. However, mysterious propaganda has been aimed at destroying tourism and trade in garments and carpets, all of which are among Nepal's main foreign exchange earners.

Nepal has a tremendous challenge in trying to preserve its sovereign independence along with its pluralistic polity. Parliamentary democracy works smoothly when there are enlightened citizenry and economic prosperity. As John Kenneth Galbraith once said, "Where there is illiteracy, there is poverty and where there is poverty, there is illiteracy." In our experience, where there are both of these vices, the survival of democracy is a miracle. They who consider democracy as a common cause should not remain silent spectators. While helping Nepal make democracy succeed, democrats elsewhere are definitely strengthening their own democratic cause.

There are no easy solutions, but a beginning could be made by setting the right priorities. For the democratic world, securing mass literacy in Nepal is the noblest of challenges. The large number of educated unemployed citizens could be employed to educate their illiterate fellow citizens. Mass literacy campaigns would result in an enlightened and organised citizenry which would help strengthen democracy in Nepal. Similarly, education would prepare people for modernisation. In this way, the country would develop its stamina to survive as an independent sovereign state consisting of an enlightened people between the two giants of the region.

VII

A Mid-Term Poll Was Inevitable—Sooner or Later

Mr. Ganesh Raj Sharma is a lawyer of repute. Armed with the unshakeable force of logic and a biting wit, he maintains a dignified aloofness from petty politics. Yet he has his own conviction transcending political borderlines. Unfazed by criticisms of his sometimes unconventional and unpopular but original ideas, Mr. Sharma enjoys an unenviable esteem for his insightful, argumentative skills and thought-provoking intellectual coherence. Metaphorically called a 'constitutional wizard' for his incessant pursuits in the field of constitutional law, he stole the limelight in the Tanakpur dispute case and also got involved in politically and constitutionally sensitive issues such as public interest, citizenship, labour, heritage conservation, the right to information, and so on.

Referring to important events such as the LAW ASIA, SAARC Law Conference held in the capital city in succession where legal luminaries from Southeast Asia and South Asia participated, Mr. Sharma fumes, "The official media did not provide coverage to the events and personalities attending the conference as well as they could". Despite his persistent reluctance, Mr. Sharma finally agreed to elucidate his views on contemporary constitutional and political issues and share them with Mukti Rijal of The Rising Nepal. *Excerpts of the interview follow.*

In the House dissolution cases registered the other day and sub-judice in the Supreme Court, what are you doing, arguing for or against?

Perhaps I will remain uninvolved. I am not going to argue for the petitioners as it is against my conviction to do so. Nor shall I appear on behalf of the respondents, since the incumbent prime minister, Man Mohan Adhikari, who was the opposition leader when a similar case was filed in the Supreme Court last year (1994), made abrasive remarks against me publicly for my academic work. Last year I placed my point of view before the court as an amicus curie. If I am requested to, I will do the same this time.

Do you think the dissolution of the House of Representatives is a prime ministerial prerogative and, if it is, should the constitutional provisions relating to a no-confidence motion not go into operation?

I may have a different political opinion than the prime minister, but I cannot deny the prerogative of the prime minister to dissolve the House and seek a fresh verdict of the people. The supremacy of Parliament is subordinate to the sovereignty of the people.

The king, according to the 1990 Constitution of the Kingdom of Nepal, does not have an unqualified right to dissolve the House. Article 53 (4) has two binding preconditions.

First, the recommendation must come from the prime minister. Second, the date of the elections must be specified, impliedly by the advice and with the consent of the prime minister. In addition, there are no other preconditions envisaged in the constitution that must be fulfilled by the prime minister. Regarding the political prudence of the mid-term polls, the king can ask the prime minister to reconsider his demand for dissolution. The king, as a consensus builder, can consult various political forces to reach a settlement. If the prime minister persists, it is in consonance with the spirit of the constitution that the king concede because the role played by the king as a symbol of national unity restrains him from entering into political conflict with the prime minister. Moreover, the court already set a precedent last year, when it ruled that dissolution was the political decision of the prime minister and could be vetted by elections alone.

Then where are the democratic and legitimate checks against the authority of the premier?

Democratic checks on the activities of the executive reside in Parliament. In addition, there is an ombudsman-type authority envisaged in the constitution though it's not effective. Only if the functions of the parliament reach a deadlock may the prime minister seek the verdict of the people through elections.

It is said that the dissolution of the parliament is an appeal to the people which the prime minister is entitled to do under the constitution. As long as the process of a democratic election is preserved, it is ultimately the people who correct errors and flaws. The parliamentary system is an imperfect system. But experience shows no better alternative to it. If a prime minister fails to maintain consensus for the stability of the government, he can go to the people with that issue. He can appeal the people to give a majority vote to his party and help form a stable government.

If a prime minister says and does so, it is, in my opinion, neither undemocratic nor unconstitutional. In this context, I would like to quote from an article titled "The Future of Democracy" published in a recent issues of *The Economist* which says, 'If democrats have spent much of the century telling Fascists and Communists that they ought to trust the people, can democrats now tell the people that this trust operates only once every few years?'

Holding too many elections is a burden to the national exchequer. Last year, we had an election and this year around the same time we are having another election. Will not the multitude of elections without a performing government give rise to a situation characterised by instability?

Ours is not a system in which people elect their rulers for a full five-year term. Sometimes, they ought to decide their position in an early or mid-term poll. In democracies elsewhere, mid-term polls, early-term polls and referendums are not objected to as vehemently as is done in Nepal. This opposition is only due to such types of elections not being a habit for a new democratic government. It is said that, in Switzerland, they sometimes hold even four referendums in a single month. Under the partyless panchayat, we had a legislative body in which legislators used to continue generally for five years. Now we have opted for a different system in which elections can happen at any time.

In Scandinavian countries like Norway and Sweden, the parliament is generally allowed to complete its term. Why cannot we poor countries like Nepal follow the same democratic tradition?

We have adopted the British first-past-the-post electoral system. In this system, the majority of votes are wasted on defeated candidates. This method provides a strong and stable government. In Scandinavian countries, a proportional representation system is adopted. Even small parties have an opportunity to get represented in the government. There are some serious problems in the proportional representation system where coalition governments often fail without getting a chance to implement their policies and programmes.

In the United Kingdom, the election system has resulted in a two-party system with a strong and stable government and a powerful and effective opposition. Nepal has opted for the UK method of election. Two major parties in this country are competing for power very effectively. It might be that this election system leads to the emergence of a kind of bi-party system in this country, too.

Let me again come to the dissolution of Parliament. There was a possibility of an alternative coalition government from within Parliament. Would such a coalition government have been a better proposition than the costlier early polls?

Forming a coalition is a very difficult task under the constitution. Even if a government could have been formed and had continued for some time, it could not have continued for a full term. A mid-term election was inevitable. Considering a mid-term election as inevitable, the three major parties vied among themselves for a government which would hold the next elections. It is obvious that contesting elections when one is in power provides an advantage in our context.

What do you think about the impartial, neutral government demanded by the opposition?

We have accepted the model of responsible government. The government is bound to ensure a free and fair election. If it fails in its democratic responsibility, it will be held accountable. By not freeing itself of that responsibility, the government must take accountability for its omissions and commissions. This was my stand when the opposition demanded the formation of a neutral, impartial government last time and this is my stand this time, too.

Lastly, how do you rate incumbent Prime Minister Man Mohan Adhikari compared to his predecessors, such as Girija Prasad Koirala and Krishna Prasad Bhattarai?

I have found that people believe that Man Mohan Adhikari is articulate, Girija Prasad Koirala daring and Krishna Prasad Bhattarai sincere prime ministers of the country.

VIII

If No Election, Recall Parliament

Nepal is currently suffering from an extraordinary situation which I have been talking about for a long time. It is based on the conflict between internal forces but also reflects regional and global tensions. There are symptoms of a proxy war with an external dimension. There have been various instances in the contemporary world when, in order to fulfil the interests of some external forces, people have attempted to whip up the internal contradictions in a country by exploring the possibilities of such conflict and then instigating it by helping one or all elements vie against each other. Such a plan is executed to squeeze out maximum concessions related to security and other vital interests without resorting to the risk of an open military operation. There are plenty of examples where such forces, guided by the objective of fulfilling their vested interests, have led the targeted country to extreme devastation and misery through their attempts to foster acute collisions among the internal forces of that country.

Unfortunately, the major political forces of Nepal have indulged in extreme hostility against each other. Regardless of the side to which they belong, Nepalis are the losers in such a situation of violence and disorder. Attempts to get rid of this vicious cycle of misfortune are still at a minimal level.

Monarchy in a Crucial Role

Nepal has a democratic constitution which was the outcome of an extraordinary national consensus that evolved more than a decade ago. Nepal has always had a highly esteemed institution of monarchy symbolising the popular consent of the people to the governance. The 1990 Constitution, too, declares that the king is the symbol of the unity of the people of Nepal. And this declaration is not merely a rhetorical expression.

Nepal is the composition of divergent natures of people integrated into one by the institution of monarchy. Now they are also consolidated on the basis of liberty and equality under the provisions of a democratic constitution. In most newly emerging republican democracies, whenever there is conflict between the army and democratic forces, as the most powerfully organised force, the army has prevailed and democracy has been sidelined. And a military dictatorship does not find any popular way to withdraw. There have been several instances in the past, in places from Korea to Turkey, in which the end of military rule has been taken as the end of the life of the person involved. But that is not the case with a constitutional monarchy. No other institution of the state appears to accommodate both civilian and military pressures and play the role of shock-absorber. Nepal itself has undergone several instances in the past when the king switched from democratic to undemocratic rule, thereby preserving the unity of the nation. The institution of the monarchy has had a significant role to play with democratic forces and the army whenever there is conflict between them. Monarchy tamps down the intolerance of the army and its desire to replace democratic forces in power. Whenever this tension builds up, the king leads the sentiment of the army and, at a convenient time, concedes to revive the democratic process with all his popularity. This has been the trend several times in the recent past (i.e., in 1951, 1960, 1979, 1991 and 2002). Now, the monarchy in Nepal has a similar opportunity to play its decisive and popular role.

Ways Out of Crisis

It is possible to overcome the present crisis if all understand its center and magnitude. Nepali people in general are still law-abiding, tolerant and peace-loving as they had the reputation of being in the past. It is obvious to all, but no major political force expresses the glaring fact that the switchboard of violence and terror in Nepal lies beyond its boundaries. Unfortunately, owing to an enormous propaganda and disinformation campaign fanned by an external center, public opinion in Nepal has been confused and divided. In the absence of a common perception of and patriotic sensitivity towards national interests, it is not possible to counter the menace the nation is facing. Likewise, without extensive awareness and consensus, there is no possibility of any kind of national unity or endeavour to tackle the challenge.

Though the centre of manipulation of the crisis appears to be elsewhere, national unity based on extensive awareness is no less important in resolving it. Those who see more and more division and discord among Nepali political forces as being beneficial to their interests will always try, visibly as well as invisibly, to drive a deeper wedge between these forces and push them towards the extreme. Although this kind of national awareness towards the existing crisis is still weak, it is where the salvation of the nation lies. The more this internal awareness grows and unity is forged, the better the chance that Nepal will overcome the current crisis. Indeed, the possibility of overcoming the present crisis is basically dependent on this factor.

If the differences among internal political forces, including the king, are narrowed down, the possibility of finding an easier way out of the crisis will increase. Unfortunately, all forces appear to be active in widening these differences. Nobody appears prepared to break down the shackles and bondage of circumstances in order to promote national unity by embracing an accommodating viewpoint and action. Possibly, none of these forces even dare to point a finger at the main reason for this crisis and have no sense of duty to end it. For this reason, there is a lack of farsighted and courageous leadership. As long as the country lacks such leadership, the possibility of ending the crisis is remote.

Election and Restoration

Was it wrong or unconstitutional to dissolve Parliament? Definitely not. The prime minister can recommend to the king to dissolve the House of Representatives and call for elections to get a fresh mandate whenever he sees there is a serious deadlock in the parliamentary exercise, and the king, too, can declare the dissolution and fresh election if the prime minister is able to persuade him of the need to do so. This was what happened this time as well. There was no constitutional mistake in this. And there was no way the Supreme Court could have deemed the action taken by the king and the prime minister as per the constitution as unconstitutional. Therefore, there is no need to review the decision of the Supreme Court either.

The main basis for the Supreme Court to call the move constitutional was the pledge to conduct fresh elections. However, when subsequent events made it impossible to hold fresh elections, the utility of the dissolution of the House of Representatives automatically ended. In this situation, the constitutional provision of keeping the tenure of speaker and deputy speaker of the House of Representatives intact, even after dissolution, certainly gives one indication regarding the letter and the spirit of the constitution. The objective of keeping the tenure of the speaker and the deputy speaker intact till the date for filing nominations of candidates for the election to the House clearly indicates that the implicit viewpoint of the constitution is such that if the elections cannot be held due to some extraordinary circumstance, the previous House under the speaker's and deputy speaker's tenures can be recalled.

One clear provision of the constitution is, without a doubt, the holding of elections. But when the situation is not appropriate to hold elections and everybody agrees on that fact, then the constitution does not envisage any situation in which the country is governed without a parliament. Therefore, it is my opinion that elections, if they can be held, and restoration, if elections cannot be held, are the best ways out in such a situation.

Indispensability of Parliament

All will be protected if the constitution is protected. As such, there should be a popular government and only such a government should frame laws. At a time when there is no way elections could be held, there is no popular, democratic and constitutional alternative that comes to my mind other than the restoration of parliament. The Council of Ministers cannot be an alternative to the popularity of the dissolved parliament, which acts as a bridge between the common voters and the government. And though the persons in the parliament may have many shortcomings, they will be refined through constant public vigilance and debate. This has been proved by the fact that, in the last three general elections, one out of every five previous MPs were re-elected by the people. Apart from this, there are no other alternatives that are constitutional. The experiments over the last eighteen months have shown that this is neither popular nor practical.

To unite the country through democratic processes, elections should be held immediately. If this is not possible, the Parliament should be restored based on the appropriateness of the constitutionally guaranteed tenure of the speaker from every angle.

Spoiled Environment

Every event has qualitative impacts. The announcement of the suspension of the elections of the House of Representatives has generated a number of anomalies. But one move to reform this step, the decision to restore the parliament, will give way to another set of positive impacts, which will in turn improve the existing political environment, which remains thoroughly spoiled. The present contradiction is unfortunately between the king and the political parties. After the restoration of Parliament, each political party will then compete with every other to gain supremacy in the next elections and thereby freed themselves from the current anarchy in the streets. One correct step will be followed by another one hundred correct steps, whereas, in contrast, one wrong step will be followed by one hundred wrong steps. One correct and constitutional decision will start a chain of many other correct decisions and will thus contribute to the cumulative effect.

A single step by the king could once again integrate Nepali politics into a peaceful, democratic and constitutional state, and this step is being anxiously awaited.

As far as controversial slogans and statements are concerned, nobody in the country has the facility or capability to put them into practice given the limitations and bondage of the hard realities of the situation within and around the country. Who raised what slogan or issued what statement hardly matters; what does matter is the limitations and bondage. Therefore, there is a need to overcome the crisis by rising above suicidal actions and reactions against each other. If there is a wish to find a way out and willingness to work towards this end, it is not impossible to keep Nepal out of the present state of chaotic and unstable politics. Many a time in history, Nepal has survived from seen and unseen imperialist designs. Now at this juncture, again the nation has to unite through the democratisation process guaranteed by the constitution.

IX

Prospect for Constitutional Reform

It is a great privilege to speak from this forum of the Council of World Affairs on the prospects for reform of the Constitution of Nepal 1962. Considering the time at our disposal, it is not possible to deal with the whole aspect of reform. I shall, however, try to bring certain basic points into discussion regarding the proposed amendment to the constitution. The first question, naturally, which haunts everybody in this context, is why there is a need for constitutional reform.

There are conflicting and varied viewpoints regarding the question and each viewpoint requires careful scrutiny, a pursuit which I may not be able to accomplish here. A section of people who considered the panchayat system as having no other alternative has also now started believing this, and the results of the referendum of 1980 have confirmed their view. They are the most bewildered people in the debate on reform in the constitution and are under the misconception that people supported the past history and status quo of the panchayat system through the referendum. At the other end of extremism is those people who are not prepared to be convinced of the efficacy of the ballot and the democratic process and want to maintain a posture of struggle in futility. Both extremes fail to understand the spirit behind the call of the national referendum and, at the same time, they refuse to understand issues from the right perspective.

The referendum was not needed to console somebody in the power that the panchayat was a legitimate political system with no alternative. This was an often-repeated slogan for about twenty years, but one which convinced nobody. What was necessary was to bring all kinds of political elements into the mainstream of national life and evolve a consensus constitutional system. If the referendum was actually supposed to have been held to legitimise what was, till the verdict, illegitimate, was it not going beyond the verdict of the people to conceive something basically new in spirit and structure from what we have at present in the panchayat system? Such people forget the conditional victory of the panchayat system, and that a very big condition of adopting that system was its timely reform. The oft-used adjective "partyless" was deliberately omitted not only from the Royal Proclamation for the Referendum but also from the yellow side of the ballot paper. The idea of reforming the panchayat system was taken in a very broad, liberal and flexible sense, for there were two equally democratic systems to choose between and when confusion came in to the debate, His Majesty the King himself clarified the matter through his message on the eve of the Constitution Day.

A marked deviation had been introduced into the political situation of the country in the last year due to the Royal

Proclamation of the National Referendum. His Majesty the King perceived and realised that to achieve a drastic change in the political system it was necessary to bring all national forces into the mainstream of national life, including those which had been separated and missed in a very tragic historic context and since then put into violent confrontation with each other. A time came when the forces in conflict, visualising the internationalisation of the struggle in the changed context in South Asia, started realising the futility of maintaining that entrenchment. The prominent among the revolutionaries jumped into the whirlwind to bring the confrontation to a grinding halt. An extraordinary consensus was achieved in an extraordinary situation, and the referendum was its grand outcome. All around, support in its favour was expressed. There was a massive mobilisation of people up to the date of polling, the majority of people maintained peace and discipline, and the content and standard of the political debate conducted inside the country throughout the period reflected the emerging political consensus. The future shape and structure of the constitution have to be moulded and cast on the basis of these considerations. The nation is at present in turmoil not because the people are impatient for any violent revolution, but because they are in search of their proper position and safeguards in the new constitutional arrangement. In this way, the debate over reform in the constitution has become a national debate. This debate has enveloped all shades of views in its fold and, for the first time in the history of this country, the common people have been involved in a serious constitutional debate. Again, for the first time in the history of Nepal, the people exercised their authority to issue a mandate for a political system of their choice. The concept of the political supremacy of the people in the form of the popular will has been incorporated in the preamble of the constitution. For the constitution to fulfill its proper role and functions, a great deal of arrangement and understanding is necessary. Without a spirit of understanding, no constitution can work.

The constitution must reflect the reality and the balance of the forces of the nation; it is not going to serve any of its purposes if, instead of a proper balance of and relationship among social forces, an absolutist view is imposed. To avoid that, it is not necessary to deal with absolutism elaborately and address each and every fragment of the society and assure its role and position; what is necessary, instead, is that the constitution be able to imbibe in it the consensus of the nation. A short and precise constitution sometimes accommodates and embraces the varied views of the largest number of its people and prevails as a universally agreed-upon political document. It is the spirit of understanding, compromise, and negotiation in the community which ensures the smooth, stable and effective functioning of the constitution. To make my point clear, I want to quote the following from the *Modern Constitutions* by K.C. Wheare F.B.A. (London: Oxford University Press, 1951: 204):

> If constitutional government is limited government, it follows that one of its enemies is absolutism of any kind. Any body of opinion and any organized movement which aims at establishing omnipotent government is clearly a force opposed to constitutional government. Absolutism appears under many names and forms—it may be called totalitarian, dictatorship of the proletariat, fascism, or nazi-ism, and it may be enshrined in a Constitution, but is incompatible with constitutional government because it claims to be unlimited and supreme. The prospects of constitutional government depend therefore on the

strength of absolutism in its various forms. As it advances, constitutional government recedes.

A chapter started in the constitutional development of this country after the referendum and democracy that is going to be the fundamental basis of the new political relationship. It has really become a watershed event in the life of the nation. Any amendment of the Constitution of Nepal has to follow the true spirit of the mandate of the people and that mandate is very clearly and categorically in favour of timely reforms. The constitution has to be reform-oriented not only to mitigate the present problems of the nation but also to maintain a continuous process of reforms too. Posterity should not face the stumbling block of a rigid constitution on the path of progress or feel the need to forcibly overthrow the order of the constitution to accommodate and bring their ideas into the political system. Incorporation of flexibility and dynamism in the polity is the aspiration of the people, as was reflected through the whole process of the referendum. All those checks and barriers to the smooth flow of reform and political dynamism have to be eliminated in the process of amendment. Repeated clarifications by His Majesty the King have furthered and assured people of the positive reform of the constitution.

After dwelling upon the theoretical premise of my argument regarding the reform of the constitution, I now want to be more precise and suggestive about the following main aspects of the constitution:

1. The rights of the people in terms of fundamental rights
2. The effective representation of the people in terms of the structure and functions of the legislature

3. The effectiveness of the institution of monarchy in terms of the preservation and consolidation of national unity, and
4. Flexibility in the process of suitably amending the constitution.

The concept of fundamental rights has a glorious history in the constitutional law of Nepal. Even before the Revolution of 1951, there were attempts to introduce political reforms and declare certain basic liberties of the people as fundamental. Refraining from enumerating all of this at the present time, I want to deal straight away with the chapter on fundamental rights in the 1962 Constitution. Article 17 of that constitution empowered the state to regulate and control fundamental rights, and the Supreme Court, through various decisions, agreed that restriction is fundamental to judicial review. Rights in the constitution are, therefore, not fundamental; on the contrary, restrictions have become fundamental. This is not a peculiar invention of the founding fathers of this constitution; it was found for the first time in Article 8 of the Constitution of the Kingdom of Nepal of 1959. This ingenuity is perhaps the contribution of the famous British constitutionalist, Sir Ivor Jennings, who came to Nepal to render his expert opinion on drafting the Constitution of 1959. The basic approach behind that misnamed provision of fundamental rights was to make the parliament all powerful. It is part of the fundamental spirit of the British constitution that the parliament is the supreme promoter and custodian of the rights of the people due to its direct accountability to the people.

Instead of relying upon the wisdom and calibre of a few nominated careerists on the bench with the power to annul an act of Parliament through judicial review, they have relied upon the representatives of the people who, through periodical elections, have an instinctive duty to remain wise and have a sense of responsibility for the preservation and promotion of the rights of the people. As the Constitution of the Kingdom of Nepal 1959 provided for a very representative, democratic and powerful parliament, they did not see the utility of double safety for the rights of the people. To maintain the supremacy of the parliament, to make it effective, and to meet the aspirations of the people, a rigid provision of fundamental rights was deliberately not created. Respecting the deep-rooted feelings of the people towards the concepts of freedom and liberty, for which great sacrifices have been made, the Revolution of 1951 was accomplished; high ideals of rights were enshrined in the constitution but they were, at best, guiding principles of the state policy. The parliament was supreme in legal terms and could ignore these rights, but ignoring them could have become very costly in political terms. The record of that parliament, due to its structure and character, was such that it did not promulgate a single piece of legislation under the safeguard of the restrictive provision of Article 8 of that constitution. The parliament, whose source of strength was the people, was always careful not to hurt the deep feelings of the people regarding their fundamental rights.

But the story behind the same kind of article in the Constitution of Nepal of 1962, the present one, Article 17, is completely different. Under this constitution, the legislature was not very effective, powerful or representative, and the rights of the people became a joke. Legislation started coming under protective clauses. Not only that, but the constitution also incorporated a new restrictive clause in its first amendment, which relates to political organisation. The previous constitution was virtually silent regarding the role of political parties and, in fact, there was not a single word about political parties or a multiparty system in that constitution, though it supposed to have provided for a multiparty system.

In the beginning, the same principle was also followed in the Constitution of 1962. Till the first amendment, the term "partylessness" was nowhere in the constitution, and it was possible to revive political parties in the panchayat system by an act of the legislature through normal processes. His late Majesty had pronounced its temporariness while introducing the panchayat system under the emergency rule and he had sought confirmation to maintain it by a resolution of the Rashtriya Panchayat, very late in 1967. Partylessness, in this way, was a casual entry into the panchayat system and not its fundamental basis. I would also like to mention here the fact of the constitutional law of Nepal that the panchayat system was launched under a constitution which was suitable for a multiparty parliamentary system. When all other provisions of the constitution were suspended, Article 55 empowered His late Majesty to promulgate ordinances according to need and circumstances and by exercising that power, he validated the functioning of the panchayat system till a new constitution was promulgated in 1962. The constitution meant to establish a parliamentary system like that of Britain. This constitution was so flexible that even a partyless system worked through it till it was abrogated in 1962. But that was possible to do only until the normal functioning of the constitution and parliament was suspended, and that was the real restraint upon any kind of arbitrariness. The 1962 Constitution was abrogated because there was no scope in it to perpetuate an authoritarian order of government. The time-tested model of parliamentary democracy had proved its worth and its capacity to ensure what is in its nature and commitment.

When the political model was changed by the Constitution of 1962, the same old position of the liberty and freedom of the people no longer had due safeguards and protections. Since then, restrictions upon the rights of the people have remained fundamental and neither the judiciary nor the legislature, due to their weak and unrepresentative natures, worked as the promoter or the custodian of the rights of the people.

While introducing an amendment, this constitutional anomaly has to be reformed, and fundamental rights have to be made meaningful and effective either through the channel of the judiciary or that of the legislature. I personally hold the view that the legislature should have a commanding strength to promote and safeguard the right of the people and, in this respect, the principle of the previous constitution has to be followed.

The rights of the people remain fundamental even if the constitution does not recognise this fact. Numerous rights of the people have yet to be recognised and, in this respect, all constitutions are, in practice, inadequate and imperfect. The mere enshrining of rights in the constitution is not enough. What is vitally important is a remedy to exercise them. There are instances in which the stronger the dictatorship is, the larger are the lists of rights without remedy. The democratic world is still imperfect in its inclusion of the most fundamental and supreme right of the people, the right to rebel if there is no other peaceful and constitutional alternative to eliminate a cruel and inhuman situation. By instinct, common people know when to resort to that right as a human being. This is not an incitement for rebellion but citing a hard-earned lesson of the constitutional law of this country developed since the Revolution of 1951. The supreme remedy lies with the people in the case that any of the wings of the state tyrannically transgress the limits of their power.

They who think that partylessness was one of fundamental elements of the panchayat system have no reasonable explanation for the role of the Back-to-the-Village National Campaign, which worked as a political party in favour of the panchayat system. In the presence of that political body, which had political functions, one can at best say that the panchayat system made ours a one-party state. But that also is subject to amendment due to the activities of several kinds of friendship and cultural associations related with various foreign powers, whose objectives have been to substitute the role of political parties as far as the preaching of political ideologies are concerned. With the help of foreign missions, freedoms denied to citizens were permitted to stooges. Patriots were silenced whereas foreign mouthpieces were free to organise and work politically under different facades of friendship and cultural associations and free to preach the theories and tactics of armed revolutions and insurrections. This undesirable situation has had several dire effects and the nation has faced chaos and situations of anarchy several times. The changing structure of the legislature and method of electing the prime minister is definitely going to bring political parties into action; however, stringent measures are to be adopted. If their political groupings are not going to be legal, the top offender of the law is going to be elected to the top position of the state executive as the prime minister.

Let the constitution not be turned into a paradise of fools. Keeping all these hard realities in consideration, one can hope, at least, that the document of the constitution will not be defaced by the word 'partylessness.' In the changing context of the situation, the legislature should have the authority to review and decide about the use and necessity of political organisations. The nation cannot afford a referendum every time there is a dispute; periodical elections to the legislature themselves can express the mandate of the people for any kind of timely reform and change. The power and process of amendment will be decisive in accommodating reforms.

The next point of my argument regards the structure and functions of the legislature. After the directive of His Majesty the King, I have a few things to suggest about the structure of the legislature and its power to control the executive wing of the state. The structure and functions of the legislature will not be fundamentally different from those of the legislature of the Constitution of 1959 if the royal directives are reasonably implemented. Once we create a very powerful and representative legislature, we cannot ignore the importance of a sober body like the upper house of the legislature. The use of the upper house is definitely for speedy control of the precipitate moves of the directly elected representatives of the people. There is a vital need for a bicameral legislature, with one house for direct representation and the other for moderation. Otherwise, a time may come when the direct representatives of the people in the legislature may come into confrontation with the king regarding controversial legislation. The upper house, or the senate, though disputed elsewhere, is very necessary in a monarchical system, especially in a country like ours, which has a bitter background of political confrontation.

In my opinion, the structure of the Rashtriya Panchayat, with some reduction in the number of representative members from districts, should remain as the upper house and it should preserve zone-based constituencies with an indirect method of election. The zone-wide constituencies have certain positive effects also in terms of integration and it is better if it is preserved with some suitable improvement. The king should have the authority to nominate a number of persons whose talents and wisdom are needed for the nation and who do not wish to enter into electioneering. Hypothetically speaking, we could let one-third of its members come through indirect elections in the 14 zones of the country, one-third be elected by the representatives of the lower house and the rest be nominated the king. Such a house will have an all-round and synthetic composition and representation in the supreme legislative functions of the state.

The lower house must be directly elected on the basis of universal and direct franchise, and each constituency should have a separate unit. There should be no nominees of the king to exhibit the distinction of representation. As the powers and functions of this body, after the royal directives, are not going to be basically different from those of the House of Representatives of the Constitution of 1959; to avoid any sentimental irritation, let this house be named the Rastra Sabha or the Jana Pratinidhi Sabha.

The role of the monarchy will be vital and key in running the affairs of the nation and, in fact, it will be a kingpin institution in the functioning of the state. The concept of the sovereignty of the parliament in the form of the king in council has a time-tested virtue and the institution of monarchy has a quite familiar precedent of working with the institutions of democracy. The king, being the supreme legal body in the constitution, has been able to act decisively in crucial moments to make the constitution effective and powerful and, at the same time, exercise restraint, too. One cannot think of other kinds of powers and positions for the king except those thought out in the constitution of 1959. The king should have all the powers and prerogatives of a constitutional monarch. At a moment of great and serious national debacle, one cannot conceive of the king like a helpless rubber stamp. In the preservation and consolidation of the nation, the institution of the monarchy has the biggest stake, and relying upon the universal attitude of self-interest, the king can be very dependable in his role. But there should be care and vigilance not to let him become a permanent autocrat. The position conceived in the present constitution does not keep that balance.

Finally, the amendment must insert in the constitution a very flexible provision for amendment. It is actually the prospect for and possibility of amendment which makes the constitution acceptable and accommodating to all. We have seen that those who swear to subvert the constitution are permanently entangled in the constitutionality of their cause. A truly democratic constitution has great integrative capacity. The 1962 constitution, by several amendments, has been made incompatible and has been disfigured. The clause governing the process of amendment has also been made rigid. It is, indeed, the rigidity of the constitution which has often forced people to look to extra-constitutional means for change in the maladies they faced and, because of this, a referendum became the only panacea. Each and every time a dreadful conflict arises, the nation and the nationalist forces will have no graceful opportunity to resolve it peacefully. The constitution must be flexible enough to inculcate in it suitable and timely changes through amending powers. Again, on this point, I look back for inspiration to Article 53 of the Constitution of 1959.

I have neither enough time nor a willingness to express myself on other provisions of the constitution. Once we accept the basic structure of the constitution as discussed above, all other provisions will have to be adjusted accordingly in that spirit. I have, on many points, cited provisions of the previous constitution, which in my opinion, is ideally designed for a country having a geopolitical situation like ours. An experiment in deviation from that constitution was launched in the name of the panchayat system and ultimately the nation was forced to decide to change its basic structure. His Majesty the King's outlines suggest amendments to the constitution which will restore all those basic elements which were in the constitution of 1959. Experience should make us not only wise but unbiased, too. Before searching for other external models of a constitution, it would be quite reasonable and prudent to consider internal aids and instruments. The country has very rich experiences of constitutional law at its disposal. The model of the constitution of 1959 was discarded not because of its failure or constitutional breakdown. The political situation in the world at that time attracted many to a model of 'guided democracy', a trend which ultimately installed autocracies and dictatorships of various kinds. As a result, the armed overthrow of systems was the only option for many people. We feel a great sigh of relief that finally reason seems to have prevailed upon the brute force of power and the culmination of the situation brought a good result in the form of the national referendum. Differences have been narrowed and the gulf has been bridged. Let the verdict of the people be honoured in a healthy spirit. The country got a very suitable constitution in accordance with the national consensus that emerged.

X

Monarchy and Democratic Development in Contemporary Nepal

As an adaptable institution, the monarchy in Nepal has been a source of change as well as a mainstay of continuity and tradition. As the most ancient of political institutions, it has passed through various stages of political development; it is as relevant in modern times as it was in the ancient and medieval periods. Though non-elective, it has always commanded the allegiance and obedience of the common people for different reasons—not necessarily coercion alone.

In Nepal, quite a large number of people believe that the king is an incarnation of Lord Vishnu. This belief of the common people has provided an impregnable emotional base for the institution of the monarchy, whose roots go deep in the political tradition of Nepal. Since time immemorial, politics and religion have been complementary to each other, and the institution of monarchy evolved in a mixed milieu. Monarchy in a Hindu polity has a traditionally religious and sanctimonious role. The coronation of a Hindu king is not only an occasion of political oath-taking, but also an elaborate religious affirmation of the commitment of the king to the people and to God. Embedded as it is in the religious sentiments of the people, it appeals more to emotion than to reason. And it is this emotion which grants the king a populism from which to rule. However, monarchy was never meant to be absolute in the Hindu polity. Limits were imposed by Vedic and similar sacrosanct religious codes that prevented monarchy from becoming absolute.

Religious sanctions and the age-old "divine rights theory" may seem irrelevant in the modern monarchical constitution, but they do not require a constitution to exist. The legitimacy of the monarchy is established by the universal recognition of its historical role as well as its capability to modernise that role. In recent times, many monarchies have come under great pressure, both internal and external, and whereas some have succumbed under pressure, others continue to exercise effective powers. The Spanish people welcomed the restoration of monarchy as soon as democracy was revived and the monarchy, for its part, has been a very powerful bastion for the survival of the democratic process in the country. The continuing popularity and legitimacy of monarchy is very much evident in war-ravaged Kampuchea as well. Prince Norodom Sihanouk symbolises the hope for freedom and independence that has enthused masses with nationalistic sentiment. But in other instances, where it has been abolished, like in Afghanistan, Iran, Ethiopia and Libya, its place has been taken by more tyrannical regimes, either of the left or the right.

One of the most glaring instances is that of the Soviet Union, where, during World War II, communists who were in power had to appeal to the people of Russia to come forward and defend the country of the great czars, recalling the contributions of Peter the Great and many renowned kings and generals. They formed military battalions and declared army medals in honour of the czars to arouse the nationalistic sentiments of the people; the influence of traditions was appreciated in the grim reality of the war.

Considering the appeal and continuing relevance of a monarchy, it is not very difficult to understand why some of the best democracies of the developed world still have a monarchy as the most respectable of all political institutions. And, significantly, this institution has the same respect and credibility in the very rich countries of Arabia as in the poor countries of the Himalayas. These facts belie the notion that the institution of monarchy contradicts modernisation.

The institution of monarchy is a stabilising force, and it maintains the continuity of the power and authority of the state. Once a country is destabilised and a monarchy is removed, there have been very few instances of stability returning. In most Third World countries, no orderly democratic system has been established after the forced abolition of a monarchy; one or the other form of dictatorship has been fighting for legitimacy against the same process of destabilisation which brought it to power.

In the past, when political ideologies had less influence than they do now, a monarchy was a factor for the emotional integration of the people of a particular territory. And at present, when political ideologies and parties represent partisan and divisive interests, the monarchy seems to have a greater relevance in embodying the common emotional relationship of a nation as well as representing integrated national consensus. In its self-interest, a monarchy, too, cannot encamp itself in a particular political ideology as it is a repository of the trust of the whole nation.

In consonance with its tradition, a monarchy at present and particularly in a country like Nepal has a goal to achieve, an ideal to fulfil. Here it has the task of institution-building as well as creating national consensus. It has to share a great deal of power with the people, and at the same time, exercise vigilance that power is not going to be used against the interests of the people by endangering the national identity. In the formative stage of democratic institutions and the nation as well, the monarch has a progressive role as a democrat as well as a conservative one as a nationalist. Maintaining a balance between these two is the most-required skill of a monarch in a country like Nepal. This paper is mainly focused on the role of the monarchy in such a paradoxical situation.

II

Monarchy in Nepal has passed through various phases of political development since the unification of Nepal in 1769. The periods since then can be divided into three major phases:

1. the period of consolidation (1769–1846)
2. the period of stability (1846–1951)
3. the period of democratic transformation (1951–present)

Between 1769 and 1846, the monarchy in Nepal, in accordance with its feudal tradition, played an active role to evolve and consolidate a political system suitable for a unified Nepal. From the small and homogeneous political unit of the Gorkha Kingdom, Nepal emerged as a multi-ethnic, multi-lingual nation-state of diverse geographical structure. In a way, it was a merger of small states, including Gorkha, that made present-day Nepal. King Prithvi Narayan Shah had to face the challenge of dealing with a vast and inaccessible country. As a visionary, he conceived of the newly formed nation as a partnership of various castes and races situated between the two great powers of Asia—namely India and China. In his well recorded directives, there are several guiding principles of state policies. In the absence of any written legal code, his directives had the effect of law. But the king was not the sole determining force in state affairs. The part played by warriors and army officers during the integration drive was also decisive during its consolidation. Because of the traditional stratification of castes by religious codes, upper-caste elites, too, had a great say in state affairs. For the rest of the common people, who seemed to have no adequate say in state policies, there evolved a body of nobles, called *bharadars,* who played the role of councilors as well as pressure groups in the political process. The Gorkha kingdom had a good reputation of rendering justice. In fact, there is still a saying that one should go to Gorkha if justice had been denied. Similarly, there was a body of councilors consisting of persons from different castes and ethnic groups. This convention was carried on in unified Nepal, too. On many occasions, the decisions of the king were affected by the pressure and persuasion of such groups. The founder of modern Nepal, King Prithvi Narayan Shah, recorded that he could not make one of his favourite persons, Biraj Bakheti, prime minister because the people liked Kalu Pande; it was this sensitivity to popular feeling which made him so successful. His "skill of leadership and vision" have been recorded well in Nepal's history.

After the death of King Prithvi Narayan Shah, the processes of consolidating the regime and evolving an administrative structure continued with a greater say of *bharadars* as successive kings were either too young to shoulder state responsibilities or were incapable of exercising influence due to their infancy. With the king as the symbol of the nation, *bharadars* continued the mission during such intervening periods with utmost dedication and loyalty to the king in power. But among themselves, there was severe competition for power, so severe that none of the prime ministers during that period died a natural death. In the rivalry for power based upon family loyalties, there were cliques of Thapas, Pandeys or Basnets coming into power by removing the other cliques in court conspiracies. The worsening of the situation culminated in the Kot Massacre, in which a large number of *bharadars*, including the prime minister, were killed. Taking advantage of the political chaos, Jung Bahadur Rana commanded the loyalty of the army with the help of his seven brothers and prevailed upon the king to procure a royal order to rule the country as prime minister. To the bewilderment of King Rajendra, his son Surendra, though still a minor, ascended the throne. In 1858, King Surendra was persuaded to issue a royal command under which all the powers of a sovereign were delegated to Jung Bahadur, leaving the king a figurehead.

That command made the office of the prime minister hereditary. That policy was renewed for each succeeding prime minister until that process was withdrawn by King Tribhuvan after the Revolution of 1951. During the Rana oligarchy, the king remained a reigning monarch without any direct access to the administration of the country. Despite this, all powers of the government were still considered to have emanated from the king, therefore his position as the source of sovereignty was not questioned by whatever Rana was in power. Terms used by historians such as "the prisoner" or "the puppet" for the king during the period do not reveal his exact position. Historical facts confirm that successive Rana rulers were acutely aware that the legitimacy of their rule depended upon the consent of the king and at no time did they even try to tamper with the institution of the monarchy. However powerfully entrenched the family may have been in the army and the administration of the country, the Ranas had learnt the lesson left by previous court conspiracies in which none of the families could continue to enjoy the support of the army once they lost the favour of the king. Thus, not relying upon their command over the army alone, the Ranas forged familial relations with the royal family and continued this trend as a strategy to ensure them power as the kith and kin of the royal family.

Besides keeping the king on favourable terms by providing stability in the kingdom and developing familial relations, the Ranas designed a strategy of keeping Nepal away from foreign machinations. Though they had allowed for the modernisation of the administration, they managed to keep Nepal isolated. With a weak China in the north and the all-pervading British empire all around Nepal, including its influence in Tibet, the Ranas aligned with the British regime in India. With this strategy, the Ranas enjoyed an unparalleled stability at home for quite a long period of time, with no external threat to their regime.

World War II was an epoch-making event across the world. After it was over, the whole world entered a reorganisation as well as a realignment of states. India's independence and the Communist revolution in China were major events which followed one after the other, making inevitable the change in Nepal. The timing and the method of change were determined by the interaction of the decisive forces related to it. The Revolution of 1951 was its natural consequence. That revolution, however, was not the outcome of any singular factor in Nepali politics. There were several factors which played a concerted role in the success of the revolution. The king was worried about reigning without the exercise of his legitimate prerogatives. Politicians who had been inspired by ideals of democracy had already launched sporadic struggles and agitations for their cause. Discord within the Rana family appeared to the surface. Prominent among the dissidents, Subarna Shumsher and Mahabir Shumsher were prepared to launch a vendetta to protest their declassed status in the Rana hierarchy. And, above all, a new power in India was in search of a viable strategy for its security concerns in Nepal. The status quo had been disturbed, as the country was soon to witness.

The new Indian government initially tried to continue adjustment with the Rana regime in the format set up by the British government by accommodating reforms. Taking the Rana prime minister into confidence, Indian Prime Minister Jawaharlal Nehru had exerted pressure upon Nepali politicians in exile to call off their agitation and cooperate with the three-tiered partyless panchayat system promulgated by Prime Minister Padma Shumsher. In a meeting on 28 May, 1947, soon after Padma Shumsher announced the basic outlines of his reforms, the head of the interim government in India, Nehru, had a very interesting conversation with M.P. Koirala and Ganesh Man Singh, both leaders of the Nepali National Congress at that time. An excerpt from the recorded advice of Nehru throws light on the strategy adopted by India towards political forces in Nepal.

> How could you assert that movement may not create more power to reactionaries? They may be bent to undertake any stringent measure and if they fall upon your movement relentlessly, this would mean complete setback of your toddling movement. If you call it off now and divert your

energy in consolidating your power, expand your propaganda among the masses, you could be better equipped for your next struggle. Calling off does not mean you stop it forever. If you find that the government is not sincere and she had not given what she declared, you could launch your movement again. Would it not be better if you let us be stronger? The Nepal government has extended her hand of friendship towards us. You know other nations are also eager to exploit her to their benefit, but India must not give that chance, she must take it. That is what I want and for this, I have suggested to stop the movement for the present. Besides, Nepal government has sent objections regarding the base of your movement in British India. To give shelter to politicians is a different thing and underground work also can be overlooked. But open bases to launch movement against one independent country is quite different thing. That is, however, significant at present but, under heavy pressure, our position will be rather delicate.

(Unpublished, in Devendra Raj Upadhyaya's collection)

Leaders of the Nepali National Congress party, the main opposition force against the Rana regime, heeded the suggestion and called off their agitation. Subsequently, the Government of Nepal Act 1948 was promulgated by Prime Minister Padma Shumsher. It was, in a way, the first written constitution apparently based on the tripartite understanding which India had initiated. This constitution was too drastic for the Ranas in power and too feeble to meet the aspirations of the political leaders. As a result, it failed without adequate trial. Ignoring this mishap, India tried to adjust with the last Rana Prime Minister as the British in India had done in the past. India, however, had kept its options open by aiding and abetting armed insurrectionists. A red-carpet welcome to

Mohan Shumsher facilitated India's entering into the Treaty of Peace and Friendship in 1950 with its far-reaching security and economic implications. Mohan Shumsher failed in his purpose to neutralize India in the internal affairs of the country by conceding what India wanted in the Treaty. The volatile situation in the north, after the arrival of the Chinese army in Tibet, had a direct repercussion in Nepal.

There is a very close link between events in the occupation of Tibet by the Chinese army at the end of October 1950 and the launching of armed insurrections by Nepali Congress insurgents in Nepal in the beginning of November 1950. Besides protesting the Chinese action in Tibet, India was in a rush to entrench itself in Nepal's strategic position. Politicians inspired by Gandhi's ideals of non-violence suggested its irrelevance in the Nepali context. B.P. Koirala narrated to this author how Nehru at that time rejected his idea of a Gandhian type of nonviolent agitation in Nepal with an outburst, "What nonsense is this Gandhism?" The Ranas in exile were already recruiting ex-servicemen of Nepali origin in India with the tacit approval of India. And the Nepali Congress party adopted a resolution in a border town in India on 27 September 1950, for an armed insurrection to be launched urgently. In a pre-arranged manner, King Tribhuvan left the royal palace to be confined within another iron gate, this time an alien one. As soon as a safe passage was managed for the king to India, an armed movement was triggered in various places of the kingdom. India was very vigilant, and it never allowed the insurrectionists to go beyond its control. It did not allow the king, the Ranas and the Nepali Congress leaders to meet among themselves and negotiate issues. The Nepali Congress leaders who were rushing to Delhi for an audience with King Tribhuvan were not permitted to see him until he had issued a call for a ceasefire, approving the reform proclaimed by Mohan Shumsher on the lines suggested by the Government of India on 8 December, 1950 (personal communication by B.P. Koirala). A "reconciliation" was imposed upon the reluctant leaders of the Nepali Congress party along with a share in the coalition government formed for an interim period. With India's upper hand in influencing the course of that revolution, it was observed by Joshi and Rose that "the decisive battles were fought in New Delhi between the Indian government and the Rana government, at the diplomatic level" (1966: 70). A question can be asked in this context: What prevented India from annexing Nepal in that situation? Some of the factors were the same as those which had prevented the British empire from expanding in Nepal. Nepal's historic tradition of independence made it difficult for a foreign power to subjugate it. Nepal's geography as well as strategic location in the Himalayas between China and India was also an important factor. Though China did not react in any way to the revolution, its military presence in Tibet certainly had a deterrent effect on India's overt involvement. As forces involved in the revolution had different and contradictory interests, another foreign power, the British government, had strong reactions during the whole turmoil. It had an interest in the stability of the kingdom because of the Gorkha recruitment facilities in Nepal. Apprehending India's strategy to prevail upon Nepal's military forces on the pretext of helping the cause of the king and the democratic forces, the Labour government in Britain, with firebrand leftist Bevin as the Foreign Secretary, had extended open support to Mohan Shumsher but regretted it when Mohan Shumsher relented to India's pressure. At the peak of the conflict between India and the Ranas, according to Daman Shumsher, "the British Ambassador had warned the Indian

Ambassador that British soldiers were to be flown from the U.K. to the capital. The very next day Indian soldiers reached Kathmandu" (1978: 112). Instead of relying upon the support of a distant ally, the Ranas, who had a huge economic stake in India's banks, industries and real estate, succumbed to the pressure exerted by India to accept a political arrangement characterised by a coalition government comprising of the Ranas and the Nepali Congress in equal ratios under the constitutional leadership of the king. Compromise within these heterogeneous political forces made the process of democracy difficult. None of the Nepali constituents had any prior experience in this process, so what occurred in the subsequent period is an account of democratic innovation and experimentation.

III

The Revolution of 1951 was a turning point not only in the political system of the country but in the concept of the monarchy. It unleashed a process of all-round transformation in society. The monarchy stepped into a new political base comprised of the popular will, identifying itself as an institution under democracy. King Tribhuvan had promised to conduct the government in consonance with the popular will. People, hence, got an elevated share in the sovereign exercise of power. Acting as a supreme element to coordinate and harmonise conflicting interests, the monarchy was temperamentally prepared for a pluralist order. Because of his initiative in the evolution of democracy and his great sense of commitment to that cause, King Tribhuvan was esteemed by the people and he, thus, aptly earned the revered title of the Father of the Nation in the sense that his reign was going to be a partnership of the people based on democratic norms.

Reality, however, was much more powerful than the wishes of the king and the people. Modern political institutions were almost non-existent. Everything had to begin from scratch. There was much antagonism among the forces which had agreed to work together. Even the process of democracy itself did not remain undisputed among committed democrats; there were differences between those with power and those without power. Since there were no elections to reach power, competition for nomination into power degraded the standard of politicians. India's role in the revolution also had made it one of the major determinants in this instability. The king had assumed his traditional prerogatives, observing democratic norms to conduct the executive and legislative functions of the state, and judicial power also emanated from him. Arriving in Kathmandu after an agreement had been signed in Delhi ending the Rana rule, the king revoked the royal command by which the hereditary post of the prime minister was conferred on the Ranas. He declared that there would be an election for the members of a constituent assembly which would write a democratic constitution. In the same declaration, he appointed Mohan Shumsher the prime minister again, but with a changed role, eulogising him as "the most trusted and loyal" servant of the crown. It is very interesting to note that the king had led a revolution for the forcible overthrow of a regime which had gained legitimacy by his own command. Excesses and abuse of power were disapproved by reappointing the same person in consensus with other forces. The king was not alone in his legitimization of the paradoxical events of the Rana regime and its forcible overthrow.

In the coalition ministry, the Nepali Congress party was led by B.P. Koirala, the home minister whom Nehru tried unsuccessfully to persuade to accept another portfolio and give Subarna Shumsher the home portfolio (personal communication by B.P. Koirala). Surya Prasad Upadhyaya, at Nehru's insistence, made his entry into the cabinet very soon after a reshuffle. From the very beginning, the cabinet lacked homogeneity of interest. In the changed situation, the Ranas had lost their decisive position as an organised force and had to depend upon the goodwill of India instead of on one or the other constituents of the agreement. Disputes among the constituents were referred to India and occasionally almost the entire team had to fly to Delhi. In the team's second such visit, B.P. Koirala was so annoyed by Nehru's sermons that he drove straight to the Nepali Embassy and asked Mohan Shumsher to return to Kathmandu immediately to resolve their differences by themselves. Mohan Shumsher remarked sarcastically that previously it had been their turn and that now it was his own, implying his newly earned favour from India (personal communication by B.P. Koirala). In a mysterious development of the situation, an attempt on the life of Koirala was made by storm-troopers organised by Bharat Shumsher with the help of the prime minister's bodyguards. Complicating these developments, the Indian ambassador was found inciting workers and students of the Nepali Congress party against the home minister (Shrestha, 1984: 166).

All the constituents were ambivalent about the position of the king, but his personal rapport with political leaders, and particularly with his home minister, was very cordial. The king, too, was unhappy with the impositions from India, the number of which was increasing with the instability at home. Each official in the key departments of the government had an Indian counterpart. In addition to that, an experienced cadre of the Indian Civil Service was appointed as the principal secretary to the king. His role was not clearly defined or specified. He was allowed to attend cabinet meetings. In one such cabinet meeting following a police firing bullets on students in which one student was killed, he castigated the home minister, alleging that "students were killed in the streets of Kathmandu like cats and dogs." (personal communication by B.P. Koirala). A huge funeral procession came out in protest, with the participation of the senior party colleagues of the home minister, putting him in complete isolation within the party as well as within the government. Koirala resigned in an unexpected radio broadcast. According to Koirala, the king was not happy with his resignation because he had developed a liking for Koirala for his defiance of external dictation. On one occasion, the king had warned him to be aware of the Indian ambassador, who had tried to create a misunderstanding between them over a letter written by Nehru, advising the king on certain personal matters. Relations between the king and Koirala were so cordial that the king had provided the home minister shelter in the royal palace when his official residence was ransacked by a group led by Bharat Shumsher (personal communication by B.P. Koirala).

In the next reshuffle, according to the terms of the "compromise" in Delhi, the Nepali Congress availed an opportunity to form a homogeneous ministry. Koirala was not excluded, as some authors imply, because he was out of favour with the king. Instead, his party formed a ministry of all the important leaders of the Nepali Congress of the previous ministry except for Koirala. A one-man enquiry commission lead by Hora Prasad Joshi was formed to investigate the firing, and it found that Koirala was personally responsible for his dismissal due to his "arrogance and incapability" (personal communication by B.P. Koirala). B.P. Koirala still hoped to get the lower ranks of leaders in the party to support his candidacy for premiership. During a meeting of the working committee of the Nepali Congress held to propose a name for the next prime minister, it was disclosed that Nehru had written a letter to the king to give preference to M.P. Koirala over his younger brother. Suspending the meeting for a while, four persons representing various factions in the party, including K.P. Bhattarai, rushed to see the contents of the letter in the palace. After reading the contents of the letter, they all acquiesced to Nehru's will (personal communication by B.P. Koirala).

Without taking such instances into account, it is not at all possible to have a realistic understanding of the role played by the monarchy in the country's democratic development. Instead of a chronological narration of contemporary Nepali history, it would be better to analyse the forces which determine the role played by the monarchy in the democratic transformation of the country. There is hardly a case which cannot be pleaded strongly, but inadequate knowledge of facts always leads to a misperception of judgement and a distortion of intent.

IV

The monarchy deserves credit for its contribution to the dawn of democracy, but in four critical junctures in the contemporary political developments in Nepal, the role of monarchy has come in for some controversy for four reasons:

- Holding elections to Parliament under the constitution promulgated by the king himself instead of holding elections for a Constituent Assembly.
- The switch to the partyless panchayat system, abrogating the multiparty parliamentary system.

- The introduction of a one-party model in the form of the Back-to-the-Village National Campaign following the second amendment to the constitution.
- The manner of conducting the first national referendum in 1980.

Political discussion in Nepal is often circumscribed by the preconceived notion that solely internal elements of politics determined the major course of political events in Nepal. There is a kind of king-versus-people misconception of these issues. In the process of democratic development, attention is always focused on how much the king conceded to the people. Attention has hardly been drawn to how much both lost to a third element—external forces. Nepal is a monarchical country, therefore there is an obsession with the British political development of the king-versus-parliament. The reality is far from that. In Nepal's peculiar geo-political situation with its dependence on one particular country, even for passage to the sea, interference by that country in Nepal's internal affairs has received little consideration. We cannot deny that there has been serious involvement of foreign powers in the internal affairs of Nepal, but it would be ridiculous to say that a country like Nepal has been a cause for concern in the internal affairs of either India or China. But, in reverse, it is a matter of concern if either of its neighbouring countries meddle in Nepal's internal affairs. For this reason, conflicts of internal interests in Nepal have a tendency to get externalized and then become alarming when meddling instigates international rivalry. The Revolution of 1951, which brought to an end Nepal's isolation from world affairs, also brought with it the beginning of international political and ideological rivalry of a serious nature.

With India's great sensitivity to its security in the north, it was prepared to go to any length to meet its requirements in Nepal, and democracy was not going to override its security concerns. Soon after the revolution, persons with no experience in state power were suddenly given the task to take on diplomatic challenges. The old fortification for self-preservation had been demolished, but a new one had not taken shape. In such a fluid situation, conspiratorial politics were bound to thrive. And, in a disorganised house like this, it was natural for a foreign power to emerge as an effective manipulator. Not taking this fact into account would render any account of Nepal's political development incomplete.

In all four of the events mentioned above, India was involved openly or in disguise. It always seems to have a double image, on the one hand, encouraging populism to the extent of anarchy and thus compromising policies while, on the other, harassing persons in power by putting them in a trap between ultra-radicals and ultra-reactionaries as they look for a loyal replacement. In the post-revolution Nepal, India has, on crucial occasions, hindered the normal functioning of a democratic process. With a little elaboration, it can be established that India harmed its interests considerably by causing instability in Nepal, by encouraging conflict between the king and democratic elements and among democrats, too. The task of democratisation in Nepal was made very perplexing. Very little attention was given to the nationalist sensibility of the people by deputing senior administrative officers from India as experts to organise Nepali administration by appointing an Indian national as the principal secretary to the king, giving him unlimited access to the government. The network of administration which evolved under Nepali tradition was being subordinated by foreign experts. India's military mission, which had come under the pretext of modernising the army, had alarmed other powers too. An organised army of insurrectionists called Raksha Dal enjoyed the pre-eminence of being ex-servicemen of the Indian Army, though of Nepali origin. Their unruly behaviour made even their political leaders unpopular. All these causes annoyed the common people and a new group of radicals germinated in politics. After the revolution, the increase in Indian activities created radicals. In a way, communism in Nepal was a gift bestowed by India in error. Communists have, since then, thrived in this country, not based on support among peasants and workers but under a slogan of non-interference by a foreign power. By arousing the nationalist sentiments of the people, the communists had been able to make a breakthrough in and even infiltrate the rigid traditional society. In this way, they were successful in forging a stable alliance with traditionalists with a long-run strategy for seizing state power from within.

Communists still have no appeal among the masses on an ideological plane. In their formative period, they had the advantage of monopolizing the bruised nationalist sentiment of the people. After gradually establishing contacts with prominent Communist powers, Nepali communists entered into a reverse role. They did not stress nationalist sentiments in relation to these powers as they did against India; in fact, nationalism was submerged under the high tide of Communist ideology. The fragmentation of international communism inevitably led to the growth of various Communist factions in Nepal and, because of their weak ideological base, they relied more on tactically exploiting the situation of contradiction between different political forces; their own positive role has yet to crystallise.

In this anomalous situation in the early 1950s, a spate of groups and factions with extreme polarisation came into being, sometimes spontaneously and many a time by secret manipulation of interested powers. The largest political party, the Nepali Congress, was also a victim of this process due to its own internal tussle for leadership. The political situation was very unpredictable; in fact, there was anarchy. An unbridled populism in the possible constituent assembly could have thwarted the very purpose of framing a democratic constitution for the country. These factors, as well as the increasing instability, drastically changed the situation, making the election for the constituent assembly irrelevant. Though Rishikesh Shaha was an early initiator of the debate, Prime Minister Tanka Prasad Acharya closed the debate by announcing that a constitution from the king himself was acceptable to the people and that holding an election for a constituent assembly was not necessary. Dr. K.I. Singh, the next prime minister, who enjoyed much goodwill, not only in the palace but also to a tremendous degree with the Indian press, also stood against the idea of a constituent assembly.

Singh's emphasis on Nepal's special ties with India had made him popular in Delhi even though he had announced the postponement of the promised general election for Parliament. His dismissal was, in fact, not as surprising as his appointment. And more surprising was the favour he was able to receive from India, which ignored the fact that he had been captured with the help of Indian troops in Nepal just about five years before being named the prime minister.

Following an agitation organised by three political parties with the involvement of the Communists, too, a date for the general election was announced by the king. An interim government headed by Subarna Shumsher was formed.

To recommend a draft of the constitution, a committee consisting of two leaders of the Nepali Congress, Surya Prasad Upadhyaya and Hora Prasad Joshi, along with another three members, was constituted. There was a broad realization of the mounting pressure on Nepal, as a result of which a consensus seems to have emerged on an early general election. The configuration of forces operating at that time makes it clear that election to a constituent assembly was essentially risky to national integrity and that it was not the king who had an interest in retreating from the promise of a constituent assembly.

The first general election for the lower house of Parliament was held under the 1959 Constitution. The Nepali Congress, quite unexpectedly, secured an absolute majority. As a leader of the party, B.P. Koirala, who alone in the party had vote-winning charisma, was nominated as the prime minister. He formed a government compromising with the heterogeneous elements of the party. Surya Prasad Upadhyaya, who had lost the election from two constituencies, was given the home portfolio with an obvious motive. Another loser in the election, K.P. Bhattarai, was elected for the most dignified of offices, Speaker of the House of Representatives.

Though the king and his prime minister did not have a similar outlook with regard to the democratic transformation of the country, the king found a common cause of nationalism in Koirala. Because of Koirala's persistence in defying terms dictated by any outside force, the king seemed to have preferred Koirala over his colleagues. The king's reason for not inviting the leader of the house to form the government was not the result of a personal dislike for him, as was believed. According to Koirala, the king delayed inviting him to form the government, mainly due to technical reasons as a relevant act was being promulgated. The king's relations with him were nothing if not intimate. The king used to delay bills and proposals if not fully convinced of their worth, but he never rejected a single one. The abolition of birta was drastic, yet it got the royal assent a year before the dissolution of Parliament. That enactment in no way affected the king's preference for the prime minister. The king did not even reject the bill on the nationalization of private forests, which left some members of the royal family and high-ranking officials substantial losers. There had been periods of pin-pricks and misunderstanding between them, to be sure, but the rapport between them had never been severed. At the final moment of the changeover, the king had given sufficient hint to Koirala that "either the king must permit the prime minister to do all he wishes, or he must pave the way for the king to have a completely free hand" (personal communication by B.P. Koirala). However, after a very cordial dinner hosted by the king, they parted company for ever. The real cause of this split was never answered by either man.

The government, which had been established with a stable election procedure, garnered a favourable response everywhere. Having a definite process of getting into power discouraged unfair competition. A sense of stability prevailed in the minds of the people in spite of the disorganisation of the party in power. Nepal's foreign relations were diversified. All major countries came closer to Nepal. The United States increased its aid programme. The Russians sent President Voroshilov as a goodwill gesture, and the Chinese preceded the Indians in inviting the prime minister for a state visit though, on India's insistence, the Nepali prime minister visited India first. The prime minister also paid a visit to Israel, where he was presented with some light arms as a gift for the Nepali Army.

This gesture, however, temporarily created a misunderstanding in the mind of the king and for India, it contradicted its conception of security in Nepal. The warm welcome accorded to the prime minister along with a peace and friendship treaty signed in China alarmed India; it worried about China's designs in Nepal. The respect shown by Khrushchev to the prime minister by inviting him to a closed dinner attended by four prominent personalities (Nasser, the Crown Prince of Morocco, Nehru and Prince Sihanouk) was an inducement to the young Koirala to compete with others for leadership of the Third-World cause. Nepal's getting prominence in this manner was not, according to India, in good taste. It was sensitive about all these developments and had a powerful and effective lobby inside the palace, ruling party and opposition parties, too. India had grievances against the prime minister as the whole thing had gone through a personal level rather than an institutional level, where India would have had great influence. Despite these grievances, India would not have gone against the prime minister had its relationship with China not deteriorated critically. As in the background for the revolution in 1951, China again was a major factor behind the events which changed the course of history in 1960.

To understand the underlying reasons for the winding up of the parliamentary process, we have to take into account the deteriorating relations between India and China and their impact on Nepal. To maintain a popular image in politics as a nationalist, Koirala was forced to correct Nehru's claim that "any aggression against Bhutan and Nepal would be regarded as aggression against India." This statement was made in the context of Nepal's denouncement of the Chinese intrusion in Mustang, a move for which the Chinese government apologised to Nepal. Koirala's statement asserting that Nepal was a sovereign nation "completely free and able to make its own decisions on any internal and external matter" convinced no one in India. Without exception, the entire Indian press was critical of the policies of Koirala, especially his equating of China and India and his contradiction of the Indian understanding of the 1950 Treaty between Nepal and India. Coinciding with the resentment in India, a wave of protests and demonstrations started coming to the streets in Kathmandu. These were similar to those in 1951 and forced him to resign under pressure. An internal feud in the ruling party added fuel to the fire. Cabinet colleagues were divided into rival factions, one loyal to the prime minister and the other to the home minister. A *dharma patra* (sacred vow) aimed against the prime minister was circulated among the members of Parliament belonging to the Nepali Congress party. It was signed by about 32 persons (Paramananda, 1982: 272). A strong voice of dissent of almost the majority of the delegates to the Seventh National Convention of the Nepali Congress was led by Biswabandhu Thapa, the party's chief whip in parliament. This was a clear embarrassment to the prime minister (personal communication by B.P. Koirala). In a similar fashion, M.P. Koirala and Dr. Tulsi Giri had issued scathing criticism against the policies of the government. There seemed to be a strange but purposeful alliance between the extreme rightist elements of the landed aristocracy and the extreme leftists under various covers, an alliance which succeeded in seeing a massive mobilization of the people to demonstrate. As the last straw on the back of a camel, Yogi Narharinath led organised violence against the police in Gorkha. Curiously, later on Narharinath also went into exile in India, from where he opposed the panchayat system. The prime minister, however, depended greatly on the information supplied by his home minister, Surya Prasad Upadhyaya, who had no sympathy left for him. When a communiqué of the home minister issued in October 1960 implicated the king in the incident, the otherwise severe critic of B.P. Koirala's policies, his own eldest brother, M.P. Koirala, after reading it, scolded the home minister, charging that he had virtually "stabbed the back of his prime minister" (personal communication by M.P. Koirala).

A source confided to this author that Nehru had used an emissary to suggest to the king that B.P. Koirala was going to create trouble both for the king and India by hobnobbing too much with China. This message was received on the eve of a warm welcome accorded by Nehru to the Nepali prime minister (personal communication). Another informed source strongly held the view that Subarna Shumsher and Surya Prasad Upadhyaya were in the first line of succession and that Dr. Tulsi Giri and Biswabandhu Thapa were in the second line of succession after the removal of B.P. Koirala. Koirala, however, was completely unaware of that fact (personal communication). It was quite clear to Subarna Shumsher that the Koirala ministry was not going to last long. The possibility of a drastic change had made the political situation very unpredictable. Just four days prior to the declaration of an emergency under the provision of the constitution, a high-ranking Nepali official had contacted Koirala with a suggestion that he discipline the provocative utterances of some of his senior colleagues in the cabinet and some members of Parliament (personal communication). The prime minister responded with a show of helplessness and requested the king to consider his precarious position. But the time had passed, and the ministry was dismissed. Had the king not acted, time would not have waited either. Some other forces would have superseded him.

Immediately after the declaration of an emergency in Nepal, under which state Parliament was dissolved, the ministry dismissed, and the fundamental rights of the people suspended, people failed to understand why Nehru was so prompt in his criticism of the king's action as the reversal of democracy whereas Subarna Shumsher, the deputy prime minister of the dissolved government, observed complete silence for more than a month while staying at his house in Calcutta.

The formation of the first Council of Ministers was delayed for almost nine suspenseful days. Meanwhile, committed democrats and radicals went into self-exile in India. There they were used in accordance with the variations in India's relationship with Nepal: they had to play the role of pacifists at one time and of terrorists at other times. No leader of any popular following was allowed to remain consistent in commitment. In due course, all of them lost their will and character as politicians. Where the repressive sticks of the regime had failed to break them, the wooing carrots offered by a foreign hand completely destroyed them, and, thus, a smooth evolution of a pluralist order was retarded.

A vast political literature has been published on this happening, but real facts are still obfuscated. As it was a serious breach of the democratic process, there have been allegations against the motive of the king for his step. Had there not been other powerful forces, which, over the time, would have overwhelmed both the institution of monarchy and the independence of the country, it would have been very difficult to understand the compulsions behind the king's actions. Koirala denied that personal animosity was a factor in his dismissal. The king had high esteem for Koirala, esteem unmatched by his esteem for any other Nepali politician. He had many admirers in India and Nehru's affection for him was great, but it was politics, and, apparently, Koirala's own high-profile personality which stood between him and others and very seriously disrupted the democratic process.

There is nothing on record from which we can infer how the Chinese reacted to this change, but the reactions of the Soviet Union, in a way, were issuing a guideline by which Nepali Communists could work. Reflecting the official view of the government, Ilya Redko, a Soviet specialist on Nepal, justified the royal action with a plea, "It became necessary because the Nepali Congress and its leadership had discredited themselves in the eyes of the people." He also compared them with "the reactionary political groups led by the Ranas" (Ray, 1983: 37). Following the promulgation of the guideline, a press release was made by D.P. Adhikari as the secretary of the Communist Party on behalf of the Communist Party of Nepal proposing a "united national democratic organisation" along the pattern of the guided democracy of Sukarno of Indonesia (*Swatantra Samachar*, 2019). What Sukarno had been experimenting with in Indonesia to infiltrate into power became a model for the majority groups of the Communist Party of Nepal, and they had a tactical split in the party with an alternative course of action under the disguise of a "pro-Chinese" label. Except in rhetoric, "pro-Chinese" exiles in India virtually aligned themselves with the Indian strategy in Nepal. For quite some time, it looked very odd that an avowedly "pro-Chinese" group was supporting an armed insurrection launched by Subarna Shumsher from his base in India. Laws were purposefully very lenient to such groups in India even during its war with China during the same period.

The mistake with India was that it thought it was alone in its collusion against the Koirala government. The aftermath of the events, however, showed that the table was going to be turned against it, too. The line followed by the British government was irritating, not just to Communist powers but also to India. A reference to Nepal in John Kenneth Galbraith's Journal is revealing.

> ...and I talked about Nepal. The Indians, as is widely known, are worried about the King who, in their view, is opening the door to the Chinese Communists and assorted local adventurers. (I had little knowledge with which to agree or dissent.) They wanted us to ask the French and British ambassadors in Kathmandu to join Stebbins in persuading the King to broaden his government. I am not very optimistic. The heads of small states must resist such pressure to show that, though small, they are independent. And the British Ambassador seems to be quite an admirer of the King. When Queen Elizabeth visited Nepal a few weeks ago, he prepared a speech for her praising His Majesty as one of the greatest and wisest since (approximately) Solomon. The Queen's managers reduced this by about a quarter and removed the part identifying His Majesty with divinity. The Queen gave that version; by accident, the Ambassador's version got released to the press. There were delighted comparisons. The Queen is said to have ordered her Ambassador sacked and then to have discovered that, as a constitutional monarch, she couldn't do it.
>
> (Galbraith, 1969: 82–83).

However powerful they are in international level, in Nepal, these powers had no basis other than in the person in power.

Whenever there was conflict, it had always been with the person in power and in Nepal, that person was the monarchy.

Before a new constitution was drafted in 1962, the then outgoing British ambassador had a significant meeting with B.P. Koirala at his detention camp, during which he discussed the importance of a reconciliation between Koirala and the king. He had offered to mediate if Koirala agreed to add content to the constitution, the title of which was to be "Panchayat," a concept introduced as per the king's demand (personal communication by B.P. Koirala). The history of Nepal would definitely have taken a more positive course had Koirala agreed to cooperate, in the manner of true statesman.

It was only after India's debacle in the war with China was reconciliation with India possible. This fact helped the king "to develop a political system based on more than a desperate struggle for survival" (Rose and Scholtz, 1980: 125). For the two preceding years, Nepal was governed by the same constitution which had run a full-fledged parliament; it was the flexibility in the constitution which endured more in an emergency state than in normal circumstances. Perhaps the king did not harbour the thought of doing away with the constitution. It was not in his interest to destroy the bridge for a possible reconciliation with democratic forces. The king was still looking for an alternative when Dr. Tulsi Giri was called for an audience almost a week after declaration of an emergency (personal communication by Dr. Giri). Biswabandhu Thapa claimed that he was the one who had recommended the panchayat scheme to the king. His recommendation, however, greatly resembled the constitution drafted by a team of Indian advisers at the time of Rana Prime Minister Padma Shumsher in 1948. Thapa had made it public that the king was not willing to outlaw political parties, yet these same people ultimately prevailed upon the king to impose a ban on political parties. Placing political parties in confrontation with the king may have been a move designed to ensure their own survival. Explaining that "New Delhi did not want to encourage populism on India's borders", Sunanda K. Datta-Ray had found in Sikkim's context that "Indian government did not trust either the palace or the politicians, but felt confident of being able to control the former" (Datta-Ray, 1984: 57). However, in the case of Nepal, India was in for a bit of surprise, for King Mahendra was no Chogyal.

Dr. Tulsi Giri had revealed in public that the draft of the panchayat-based constitution was given to Jayaprakash Narayan (in India) and Surya Prasad Upadhyaya for perusal. After its promulgation, India's attitude towards the new constitution did not appear hostile. It was more concerned with the details of implementation than other concerns. In his account, India's former ambassador found "the direct democracy at the base and indirect elections upward", as designed in the constitution, in consonance with Gandhi's ideas (Narayan, 1971: 81). In an atmosphere of cordial relations with India, and with Surya Bahadur Thapa as prime minister of Nepal, the first amendment of the constitution was promulgated with the term "partyless" inserted for the first time. The response was an overwhelming acclamation of all shades of views and lobbies in the panchayat. That was a heyday for Indian influence in Nepal until an incident occurred at the Kathmandu exhibition ground when the Chinese issued a threat to "break skulls of Nepali reactionaries, Indian expansionists and the U.S. imperialists in the streets of Kathmandu" (Ray, 1983: 78). That perhaps is the worst ever threat issued against Nepal by the Chinese for its too close ties with India as well as the West. In open defiance of the law in

Nepal, revolutionary "red books" and lockets of Mao were distributed freely by a new group of radicals tutored in the thoughts of Mao Zedong. This incident cautioned Nepal that there was a limit to the government's yielding to the pressure of any one power in the region. The political system of the country naturally reflects this reality. There had been a compelling situation for a readjustment in the context and structure of power in 1975, a fact which resulted in the second amendment. A change of that magnitude had occurred in the region after the bifurcation of Pakistan in the east. So that it would face no humiliation, like the war with China in 1962, India entered into a "peace and friendship treaty" with the Soviet Union on similar lines to the treaty that brought Soviet troops into Afghanistan for the "rescue" of President Amin. After the American withdrawal from Vietnam, the balance of power further shifted in favour of the Russians. Bangladesh's birth was the success of the Indo-Soviet alliance in the region. "Operation Sikkim" changed that status of Sikkim's independence. Elected representatives of the people were made instrumental in endorsing a merger with India whereas the Chogyal of Sikkim did his utmost to preserve the identity of the nation as a testimony to the fact that nationalism was not only an ideal to opt for but a precondition for the survival of the monarchy in a country. Internal political dissension in Nepal had gone to the extent of calling for an armed insurrection from a base in India, and the Panchayat had also experienced rampant opportunism and indiscipline in a struggle for positions of power. In this unnerving tension and turmoil in 1972 came the sudden demise of King Mahendra, a visionary and astute leader of the nation. His son, King Birendra, at the age of 27, then had to suddenly face a volatile situation before he had a chance to perfect his political apprenticeship. To conduct the affairs of the state afresh, the king had rightly encouraged pluralism in panchayat forums, and he himself changed the style of addressing the people, which was wrongly perceived as a weakness. Instead of reciprocating his gestures, even senior leaders of the panchayat took refuge in extreme populism by alleging the existence of "parallel administration of the government and the palace". Under the cover of popular leadership, the call for an armed insurrection from a base in India appeared to pose a "Bangladesh" type of threat in Nepal (Raina: 1981: 48). Without the awareness of Ganesh Man Singh and without much effort on the part of B.P. Koirala, there had been a major attempt at insurrection in the eastern part of the country, in Okhaldhunga. To encounter all these threats and challenges in a political manner and to maintain external and internal peace, the king declared his desire to amend the constitution. Sribhadra Sharma and D.P. Adhikari, from the Nepali Congress circle and pro-Russian Communist circle respectively, were included in the committee for drafting the second amendment to the constitution. But there was no effective leadership on the popular level to explore the possibility for broad-based accommodation; nostalgia for "total revolution" seems to have made politicians prisoners of their own imaginations. As the national debate had been launched to evolve a model for change, there was an abrupt suspension of democratic procedures with the declaration of emergency rule in India. Whatever logic Mrs. Indira Gandhi extended in her self-defense, it had a direct message to the protagonists of the hard line in the panchayat.

A section of the panchayat leadership who were interested in a stringent process with a one party-like system which would ultimately confront the king for power on the issue of ideological formulation, cadre control and programme implementation began to emerge as a force. A structure of leadership "following the Leninist blue-print of party organisation" (Shaha, 1978: 217) was designed with a greater scope of alliance with pro-Russian elements. Before realigning with Russia, Man Mohan Adhikari had revealed that Russia had demanded a say in the government as well as in the political leadership of their followers in Nepal, in return for which "the Soviet Union would support the king to the hilt" (Kumar, 1984: 63). In India, a school of thought known by the name of Kumarmangalam had advocated, inside the Indian Congress Party, a one-idea state to have a committed administration and judiciary in order to achieve socialistic goals. This principle served as a guideline for the Indian government at that time. Leaders from Nepal, dependent on India, were greatly influenced by this doctrine . Therefore, it is not surprising that, apart from some sections of the Communists, even the leaders of the Nepali Congress associated with Subarna Shumsher, individually and collectively, welcomed the amendment with the expectation that they would get a proportionate share in the hierarchy of the leadership in the Back-to-the-Village National Campaign (BVNC). The selection, however, was very disappointing to them.

Frustration developed gradually among all, including those who had opted for the system but were unable to function as a political party. Such people, who had got key positions, wanted the political power of the king transferred to them to advance the cause of the panchayat system. But it was not in the interest of the king to strengthen authoritarianism, for it would have been a repetition of the folly due to which the Rana regime had come into existence. Having a monarchy and a one-party system is not only antagonistic but is also an impossible idea. Partylessness permits pluralism in ideas, and monarchy is in harmony with such pluralism.

The king's wish to experiment with a disciplinary body in the panchayat led to a disastrous confrontation with his own authority. Persons nominated to various levels of leadership did not have the capacity or the popular support to withstand the crisis generated by the agitation of "students"". In fact, this was a smokescreen for contradiction among themselves and irreconcilable differences among divergent loyalties. If there was a serious struggle to capture positions of power, their failure to control the organisation from within induced them to ignite an explosive situation in the country, a situation which was diffused only when the king intervened with his call for a referendum. The people rejected the authoritarianism of the BVNC as they saw it inconsistent with the larger interest of the monarchy. And the referendum itself was the culmination of various forces, both internal and external, that got linked in an unusual manner.

It is generally believed that the referendum in Nepal was necessitated by a "massive student agitation". This illusion, particularly among politicians, has done incalculable damage to the democratic development of the country. Off and on, politicians in later phases issued threats of a show-down like the one the people engaged in in 1979. In that delusionary picture, agitations were launched but aborted repeatedly due to compromise elsewhere. It is, indeed, possible in the world today and particularly in "soft states" to create agitation and destabilise the power structure with an external force having an advantageous geographical position and enormous resources at its disposal. The technique of various kinds of propaganda and disinformation can be used systematically to arouse public resentment and dissatisfaction. Or the passive discontentment of the people can be fomented into a revolutionary outburst. And, amazingly, the whole show remains under the control of a mastermind behind the screen. Masses on the streets and leaders with populist stands are manoeuvered as a proxy-troop to achieve a goal. In the name of the student agitation, this manoeuvering happened in Nepal. Otherwise, how on earth could an agitation having purely academic issues in the charter of demands accomplish a dramatic change which no political party had ever envisioned? Students were saluted from the public platforms addressed by leaders of prominent political parties for having awakened them from the "slumber of political inactivity". Almost the lone exception was B.P. Koirala, who branded the turmoil as the act of anti-national forces seeking to endanger the national existence. But so-called "pro-Chinese" politicians like Man Mohan Adhikari were on record saying that it was a spontaneous upsurge of the people and that they were satisfied that India was not implicated in the turmoil for the first time (Kumar, 1984: 172). Though he himself was involved in inciting people for it, Ganesh Man Singh saw "a national and international conspiracy" (against Nepal), indicating that India and the Soviet Union were behind the uprising. Elaborating the point, he said:

> It is the government of India that has been all the time obstructing, preventing and standing in the way of the Nepali Congress. May I tell you that Nehru was angry with King Mahendra not because he (the king) dismissed democracy, but it was "for something" else. All the time, in the case of all the prime ministers in Delhi, and the government of India all through, this is the policy that prime ministers in your country have been following of not

> letting Nepali Congress getting the upper hand. What is being done is to alternatively push it (Nepali Congress) up and then after boosting it, bring it down. This is the way the "big brother" functions: that is how the "big brother" wants the king and the "democratic elements" to sit on the negotiation table and reach settlement. This has always been India's attitude—to interfere, to push down the Nepali Congress and then to make the king and Nepali Congress sit together on the negotiation table. Ever since 1951-52, India has been doing this.
>
> (Kumar, 1984: 49–50).

It is interesting to note that the "student agitation" of 1979 is not an isolated incident occurring in an isolated country. It coincided with the overthrow of the Shah regime in Iran and the Russian occupation of Afghanistan. Whether a similar situation would have occurred in Nepal on its own is difficult to say but to deny any external design is rather a poor comfort.

Things are shrouded in mystery, but various inferences and conjectures can be drawn regarding the royal declaration for the referendum to enable people to choose between a multiparty system and the panchayat system with suitable reforms. The visit of Dinesh Singh as an emissary of Indian Prime Minister Morarji Desai and his audience with the king also has to be taken into account (Kumar, 1984: 30). The referendum could have been a plausible measure to diffuse the turmoil which foreign powers may have played a prominent part in creating. If this interpretation is valid, it would be like a reconciliation similar to that of 1951, in which a person loyal to the king and trusted by India was put into a key position with the rest of the dissenters occupying the public platform for multiparty propaganda.

Whatever might have been the reality, the royal declaration for the referendum did not stop violent incidents in the far and wide corners of the kingdom until Surya Bahadur Thapa, who had almost been in oblivion and had no popular image either in the panchayat or among the agitators, was unanimously recommended by the Rashtriya Panchayat for the office of the prime minister. It was perhaps the first time since 1951 that the appointed prime minister was not able to declare a list of his cabinet colleagues for about three days, likely due to hard bargaining over the allocation of key portfolios. Then, there followed a series of resignations and replacements of persons in various strategic departments of the government.

It is not known what role Research and Analysis Wing (RAW), an intelligence agency formed to influence the politics of the neighbouring countries of India, played during the upheaval in Nepal. Developed as a highly skilled institution, it had not briefed even Mrs. Indira Gandhi, the then prime minister of India, twenty-four hours before commencing "Operation Sikkim" in the process of Sikkim's annexation (Raina, 1981: 64). What it was doing in Nepal may not necessarily have been known to the leaders of the Janata Party in power. In the absence of conclusive proof, a little bit of logic can help one reach a conclusion. At the time of the royal announcement, India lacked a homogeneous leadership; it was faction-ridden with several over-ambitious persons out to grab power. Within a year of the declaration of the referendum in Nepal, three different political parties had succeeded each other in power, one after the other. By the time polling for the referendum had begun in Nepal, Mrs. Indira Gandhi had emerged in India to reverse what the Janata Party had done. There was, therefore, a new approach again in India with regard to Nepal. In the meantime, the Russian army had crossed the traditional boundary of South Asia in Afghanistan, thereby endangering India's superiority as a regional power. All these dramatic events changed the original context of the referendum. After completing a full circle, India again realized that the panchayat system was the only alternative for stability in Nepal, a state which was essential for India's stability too. There had been a misconception among many that the multiparty side would muster much support among the people had B.P. Koirala combined all anti-panchayat forces together. There was gross ignorance about the composition of the anti-panchayat forces, a large number of whom were activated by strings elsewhere. As there had been a clear clash of interests in Nepal between the Communist bloc countries and India, however alike they appear, a unified opposition with a long-term common strategy was a mistaken idea. Inside the Nepali Congress leadership, persons like Surya Prasad Upadhyaya preferred to join forums with either Communist leaders like Dr. Rayamajhi or autocratic-minded Communists like Dr. K.I. Singh than to join forums with their own senior party colleagues. Even B.P. Koirala's close associates, such as Ganesh Man Singh and K.P. Bhattarai, lacked an identical stand during the referendum. And, it was not difficult to find external forces behind disruptions in the anti-panchayat rank. India's strategy had been to create pressure to make moderates in the panchayat acceptable. Had a person like Thapa not been accommodated in power, a next round of turmoil was imminent. How handicapped the opposition forces in Nepal were by their dependency on external forces was diagnosed by Lok Raj Baral in an earlier but similar context:

> From the opposition point of view, the influence of both China and India on different opposition groups is becoming

> equally determining factor in many respects. For the period under review showed that the oppositional elements i.e., formal political parties, were mostly divided among themselves on their ideological allies—China and India. While growing pro-Chinese and pro-Indian feelings considerably helped this process of the disorganisation of the political forces, this proved to be congenial to the consolidation of the Panchayat System.
>
> (Baral, 1977: 179).

The position of the panchayat side in the referendum was very anomalous. Unlike the outlawed political parties, it had no political organisation. The network of the BVNC was dissolved soon after the announcement of the referendum. To propagate political views freely either way, laws were relaxed by a royal declaration by which politicians were able to reorganise their cadres in the manner of political parties. The panchayat side had also an ad hoc body to conduct campaigns for it in competition with other political parties. Within the parameters of the panchayat system, the referendum was virtually an exercise in multiparty politics. A search for an alternative political order was permitted to the people. The element of popular consent had a chance to evolve an accommodating political system. The panchayat had a discredited liability of power for a long period. The most appealing points in the panchayat's favour were the stability and deep sense of Nepali nationalism it provided under the active leadership of the king. The multiparty side had miscalculated the appeal that the monarchy had among the people. Even hard-core Communist leaders like Man Mohan Adhikari had to declare publicly that they would support the stability of monarchy as long as the temple of Lord Pashupati Nath was present. But mere rhetoric was not going to convince the masses to embrace a drastic change in the political system and the traditional support which the monarchy commanded. These were the key factors in the panchayat's favour.

VI

Knowledge of history has no use if it does not impart wisdom. The history of Nepal and particularly its period of democratic transformation must make both the king and the people wiser. Nepal's history has a geographical imprint on it; being sandwiched between two great powers of Asia, it has an advantage when both are balanced in strength. Having a weak neighbour on either side has never been in Nepal's interest. It is, therefore, not in Nepal's interest to play off its two neighbours to weaken the equilibrium. This situation does not permit Nepal to be an appendage of either neighbour. Whenever it has aligned itself with one, it has caused tension between the two neighbours; this is a historical reality which both powers have to keep in mind.

Preservation of Nepal's own identity and promotion of popular aspirations were highly interrelated during this period. Stability as well as change have to be entwined through a continuity of power. The monarchy is the only institution which can be conceived of in both a traditional and a heterogenous nation. The inherent capacity of this institution to survive historical upheavals is derived from the religious and cultural sanctions of the society. Even democratic reforms need the legitimisation of this institution. The monarchy in Nepal has a tradition of leading the nation during epoch-making moments; some Nepali kings are remembered as persons of vision with the will to change the course of history. As a visionary, King Prithvi Narayan Shah was able to formulate a far-reaching strategy in his drive to create a unified nation.

The Kingdom of Gorkha was not a viable state to survive long until Shah enhanced its strength by integrating several small kingdoms which, on their own, were vulnerable. He inspired a dream into his army to unite several smaller states into the great kingdom of Nepal. As the dream was realistic, he succeeded.

King Tribhuvan carried out his leadership in exemplary fashion by establishing a democratic order in Nepal. He conceived of a change and formed a common cause with the modernizing ideals of the democratic elements of the country before there was any ray of hope of a democratic revolution. The Ranas, who found him hobnobbing with revolutionaries in 1940, had no alternative but to live with him with greater vigilance; he was, however, invincible in his zeal. But for his commitment, there was hardly any chance for democracy to strike root in the country, even after the termination of the Rana regime.

Another legend in the tradition of monarchy was King Mahendra, who, through his ideas and performance, played a very controversial role in Nepal's history. A dispassionate assessment of his role leads to the conclusion that, without abandoning the basic ideal of liberal democracy, he had the audacity to initiate an alternative political system suitable for national conditions. As Nepal had never been under colonial rule and had not engaged in prolonged hostility against any foreign power, a sense of nationalism had not yet been fostered as a modernising ideal. King Mahendra imparted a multi-dimensional quality to the newly emergent nationalism, which was not merely political but also manifest in the social and cultural lives of the people. He saw it as a question of national survival. Through his unwavering stand, King Mahendra emerged as a true nationalist in Nepali history.

It is too early to fully assess King Birendra in his continuation of the noble tradition of monarchy in Nepal. Before ascending the throne, he had had sufficient academic briefing on the problems of development in Third World countries with special reference to Nepal. During his apprenticeship in power, he formed a conviction that development was a human problem related to attitudinal changes in people. Adding a new cause to his mission, he emphasised that balanced economic development do away with regional disparities in the country. He seems to have focused his efforts on promoting nationalism, democracy, and economic development. The greatest achievement of King Birendra is that he has been able to command all-round respect and confidence from all walks of life. As a person, he is free from the aspersions to which rulers of the Third World are often subjected. His political norms are ascertainable and his behavior, predictable. He has been able to generate new hope through his commitment and dedication. The monarchy he personifies is a great hope for the development of a modern democratic order in the country.

The difficulty with foreign viewers of Nepal is that their perceptions develop in their respective political environments at home. Persons from a society which had the experience of struggling against an alien rule and subsequently ended up in a republic try to compare their experience to that in Nepal, where there was no struggle against any such enemy. Preachers of class struggle, similarly, trying to fit a cap on the wrong head in Nepal, enflame a non-existent conflict to flourish. The country and its problems must be viewed from the correct perspective, a task at which outsiders often fail. The performance of the monarchy cannot be judged properly from a republican ethos. Nepal is in a very precarious position geographically as well as politically. On both sides of the country, there are irreconcilable political systems and it is very difficult to resist their pressure. But neither of the political patterns dominating these divergent systems of governance can help Nepal to maintain its equilibrium.

Democracy is a process which can neither be imposed by law nor imported from abroad. Even a revolution stands in the way of democracy after revolutionaries capture power and seek to monopolise it. Democracy evolves gradually at a speed which is irritatingly slow. It is impossible to bring about a change of power overnight by the will of the sovereign or by force. Democracy depends on incessant practice. The more it is practised, the more it is strengthened, but it must not be strained or stretched beyond the objective conditions of the country concerned. It would be a great folly to overlook what Nepal has already achieved on the way to democratic polity. Compared to the situation before 1951, a revolution has taken place in building the infrastructures for democracy, except, of course, the formation of political parties based upon the interest aggregation of the people. Whatever might have been the form of government, there has been a cohesive process of minimum democratic norms in the country since the Revolution of 1951. There has always been one or another form of popular representation in the government to aid and advise the king to conduct the affairs of the state. There has always been a hierarchy of courts in the judiciary with adequate safeguards of tenure and emoluments to make it impartial and independent in disputes between the state and individuals as well as among individuals. The Supreme Court has earned a great deal of trust from and the regard of the common people even in the remote parts of the country by its extraordinary powers such as habeas corpus and other prerogative writs which are popular in other democracies.

The decisions of the Supreme Court have the force of law as precedents, and, in a very short period, the court has made rich contributions to the development of constitutionalism. Acknowledgement of the positive aspects of democratic development does not rule out the retardation which the process has suffered during the period. Enough has been enumerated in the appraisal of the situation mentioned above. There is, however, no full stop to the process of democratic transformation of a society. The process of modernisation, which has so lately been initiated, has released forces for an all-round change, including attitudinal change.

VII

In the politics of the region, there have been spectacular changes. A movement for rapid modernisation with openness though within the framework of one-party rule has already moved ahead in China. In India, a new generation of leaders with a fresh outlook seems to have assumed the task of speedy economic development, preserving intact its democratic institutions despite the strain unleashed by forces of destabilisation. India's Peace and Friendship Treaty in the nature of a military alliance with one particular superpower is already showing signs of strain. There is a marked deviation in its regional and global attitudes. The initial distrust towards the South Asian Association for Regional Cooperation (SAARC) has been modified with its commitment to regional cooperation. This is evident from Rajiv Gandhi's description of SAARC as "the democracy of the countries of South Asia", which is certainly not mere demagoguery. For the first time in history, leaders of the region have been able to establish a forum in which to sort out bilateral problems informally and multilateral concerns officially. The direction taken by the regional parley is, indeed, very promising.

In such a changed regional context in Nepal, the institution of the monarchy has to build up a consensus at home and sympathy abroad, particularly as there is no other dependable leadership in the country. A working relationship between the king and the people is certain to crystallise with all the attributes of a liberal democracy as understood in our part of the world. It is neither possible for the monarchy to withdraw into a wishful status quo nor for the people to preserve the independence of the country without the support of a monarch who is charismatic and traditionally regarded. The independence of a country is sine qua non for the freedom of an individual; loss of the independence of a country will result in the loss of the freedom of the individual. Along with the independence of the nation, the monarchy in Nepal in the present context has made democracy and economic advancement its twin goals.

The need for evolving a democratic relationship is, therefore, a consensus stemming from rational self-interest without much strain and stress. People who do not agree with the prevailing political system on ideological grounds still have the greatest of democratic rights—the right to dissent. The right to organise dissent is well-developed in practice. The right to express different views and ideologies, except for restrictions imposed by the enactments of the legislature, is guaranteed by the constitution.

Political activists hostile to the panchayat system participated in the general election. However, the constitution prohibited groups from functioning like political parties under the "partyless" system. A kind of pluralist activity, which was permitted within the forums of the panchayat, has gained momentum in the present environment and has tempted adherents of the multiparty process to participate covertly in the Rashtriya Panchayat and overtly in local panchayat elections. The way the Rashtriya Panchayat functions and the freedom of speech exercised in the House have a reassuring effect on the democratic opinion of the country. There are resentments, however, and they will exist for a long time to come. But there should be a clear distinction between genuine and popular grievances and unreal and manipulative grievances. The king at this moment is destined to play the role of a supreme arbiter. But that power is not to be used arbitrarily; there is no scope in the constitutional system for an absolute monarchy in Nepal. The Constitution of Nepal has provisions for democratic checks and balances which have yet to be strengthened by practice and healthy convention. The constitution lays out the powers and prerogatives of the king, making it clear he is a constitutional monarch. More could be developed in a peaceful and constitutional process by consolidating the political freedoms guaranteed by the constitution. This is, certainly, a system with adequate room for changes for the better.

Debates regarding different alternatives to the panchayat system were not brought to a close by the result of the 1980 referendum. That result has left its impact on the process and manner of conducting the politics of the nation, but ideas and convictions in people's mind could not have been effaced by it. A considerable proportion of the population, especially urban-centred elites, have not been fully reconciled to the results of the referendum, though they do admit to the ample democratic principles in the functioning of the panchayats. Similarly, debates about different alternatives within the panchayat framework are also underway. The way the various panchayat function has not been a matter of full satisfaction to anybody. There is no legal barrier to holding debates about alternatives within or outside the panchayat system openly and freely. Stringent laws were either relaxed or amended after the referendum to facilitate considerable freedom of expression. To preach an idea against the panchayat system is not only an academic freedom; this freedom is much in practice, too, and to advocate the cause of multiparty or other pluralist concepts is also permitted by the law. The only restriction is upon organised efforts to capture the government on the basis of any ready-made ideology.

The partylessness of the constitution has not been strictly defined in law; holding various views individually or in groups or associations is, therefore, permitted. Partylessness in practice cannot be equated to totalitarianism; there is a degree of freedom of thought and expression in the law of the land. If is exercised in the spirit of promoting and strengthening democratic ideas and institutions, there is no reason why the law should be a stumbling block. But that is not happening here. The feelings of people are rarely represented by political parties or the media and a sense of social responsibility is quite lacking in both the media and parties. Opportunities come for momentary upheavals, and politicians fall prey to them. Powerful political factions with extraneous loyalties have emerged in the liberalised scenario in the country. The valuable freedoms of the people, guaranteed by the constitution and protected by the judiciary, have become subterfuge to them. In their denial, the image of the nation is tarnished. Such cliques not only control organisations and the media in Nepal, but they also manipulate the opinions and judgements of the people, too. Journalists of long-standing reputation can hardly compete with the organisations and resources of offshoots in the media which appear in giant proportions to sensationalise events. Similarly, politicians are built up overnight with greater mass appeal and charisma than those who have spent the best part of their lives dedicated to their mission. But these lifelong politicians, too, seem to have lost their sense of direction and political grit. Leaders in their respective organisations have become mere show persons who are neither elected by delegates of the party nor accountable to any formal bodies within the party. Cadres seem to have lost their right to elect leaders and instead choose political lines forever. They are not aware of their party's rules, and they are just at the mercy of an invisible hand inside the party which seems to have taken leadership. Whatever resolutions come out in public are prepared, not by a leader or committees in conventions, but behind closed-door chambers of unknown centres. These resolutions, therefore, usually disregard the consensus within the party. Every party activist, in confidence, expresses his helplessness; but in public, as a careerist, he speaks differently. Running a political party in a poor, illiterate and traditional society has not proved to be a successful democratic exercise. Even if a few handfuls of idealists in such parties are aware of the malady, they are not capable of reforming this ill, for they require patronage to survive in an unresponsive society. In a desperate attempt to continue their career, they compromise and live with the evil.

Money has always been a very powerful source through which political power comes, and that is very much applicable at present in Nepal. It is almost impossible for an honest and patriotic person to solicit support for his views in public because influencing the media and contesting elections requires enormous resources. Even government-backed candidates have not been able to mobilise the amount of resources which persons with a "proletariat theme" have recently been able to acquire under publicly known patronage. It is a common practice in all major countries to patronise and subsidise various friendship and cultural associations, but some one-idea states have used these as forums to propagandise their respective state ideologies. Hence, under diplomatic protection, their local dependents exercise more political freedoms, even to the extent of injecting violent revolutionary doctrines in the raw minds of teenagers.

On many occasions, officials of internationally ill-reputed diplomatic missions having links with international terrorism have been found involved in the smuggling of various goods and in the trafficking of drugs and their names have been recorded in the confessions of their co-accused. In that way, local money is raised with a clear purpose of financing "revolutionary" persons, and the media serves as their vanguard. Obviously, that pooled money has every chance of being used in panchayat elections, making elections undesirable and costly. Some diplomatic missions have permitted their local policy-preachers to sell scholarship grants to prestigious learning centres to raise funds for their local activities. Instead of admonishing such nefarious deals, the media popularises them as championing the rights of the people. And, the government is always prompted to do a balancing act between the parties to mitigate serious destabilisation; in that process, every party is left to counterbalance the others.

In this undesirable state of affairs, the country is experimenting with a liberal democratic system based on direct adult franchise with an assurance of optimum fairness in elections. In a situation in which even God might fail, the monarchy is preserving national identity and promoting democratic ideals. Here, in this connection, the trust and belief of the common people in the monarchy is a strength which can generate hope for both.

Preserving national independence is in the interest of the institution of the monarchy, without which the country would have lost its existence as an independent and sovereign state. The history of Nepal testifies that the monarchy symbolises the nation.

The monarchy has come a long way in its commitment to democracy, which has taken shape in various institutions. However hazardous the task, the monarchy has, in no way, retreated from the democratic process that has already been initiated. Democracy, in its full sense, has become a goal in Nepal, and the institution of the monarchy, at present, appears to be the best guarantee of its meaningful implementation.

References

Baral, Lok Raj, 1977. *Oppositional Politics in Nepal.* New Delhi: Abhinav Publications.

Dutta-Ray, Sunanda K., 1984. *Smash and Grab: Annexation of Sikkim.* Bombay: Vikas Publishing House.

Galbraith, John Kenneth, 1969. *Ambassador's Journal: A Personal Account of the Kennedy Years.* Boston: Houghton Mifflin Company.

Joshi, Bhuwanlal, and Leo E. Rose, 1966. *Democratic Innovations in Nepal.* Berkeley: The University of California Press.

Kumar, D.P., 1980. *Nepal: Year of Decision.* Bombay: Vikas Publishing House.

Narayan, Sriman, 1971. *India and Nepal: An Exercise in Open Diplomacy.* New Delhi: Orient Paperbacks.

Paramananda, 1982. *The Nepali Congress Since Its Inception.* Delhi: B.R. Publishing Corporation.

Rania, Ashoka, 1981, *Inside RAW. The Story of India's Secret Service.* Vikas Publishing House.

Rana, Daman Shumsher, 1978. *Nepal: Rule and Misrule.* New Delhi: Rajesh Publications.

Ray, Hemen, 1983. *China's Strategies in Nepal.* Radiant Publishers.

Rose, Leo E., and John T. Scholz, 1980. *Nepal: Profile of a Himalayan Kingdom.* Boulder: Westview Press.

Shaha, Rishikesh, 1978. *Nepali Politics: Retrospect and Prospect.* Bombay: Oxford University Press.

Shrestha, Kusum, 1984. *Monarchy in Nepal.* Bombay: Popular Prakashan.

Swatantra Samachar, Vikram Era 2019, Asvin 19.

XI

Nepal's Political Crisis: Regional Perspective

There is unanimity of opinion about the political situation of Nepal: that it is alarmingly complicated and, thus, getting out of hand. The difference in belief regarding the cause of that complicatedness, however, is very wide. Some people, forgetting that the previous constitution was scrapped with a hope of salvation by a new one, find fault with the constitution. Some people believe that the expensive procedures of elections are to be blamed as the source of all evils. The nation still remembers the less expensive and unfair elections of the past. Some people argue for the direct election of the prime minister as the chief executive of the state with a fixed tenure, believing that this practice would ensure a stable and effective government. Recent events in the Philippines, Indonesia and Peru belie those expectations. In contrast, India has a prime minister leading a coalition of 13 political parties with heterogeneous commitments, who is confident about holding another election after completing his full term. Some people believe that the deterioration is due to the lack of a visionary prime minister. President Junius Richard Jayewardene of Sri Lanka was an outstanding leader with a convincing vision to see his country reach the level of development of Singapore within a decade. He had to leave his responsibilities without success amidst a dreadful civil war in which about a dozen politicians of outstanding calibre and tens of thousands of others were killed. And, Nepal has its own experience in the matter. K.P. Bhattarai, who was given credit for magical success as an interim prime minister during the transition in the country from the panchayat system to multiparty democracy had to quit in utter humiliation during his second term as prime minister. One has to take into consideration, therefore, all visible and invisible factors and trends while analysing the political situation of the country in its entirety.

For decades, the country has been suffering from the effects of political instability. All basic infrastructures of the state exist, but they do not seem to perform well. Politicians, a motley crowd who have been elected to lead the nation at enormous cost, seem to have lost their way in a dark forest. Leaving aside the job assigned by the people, they have become like captive agents who further destabilise the country under the machinations of an unseen force.

The constitution envisages a prime minister having carrots and sticks in his hands to provide a democratically strong government. By an authoritative interpretation, he has been turned into a shuttlecock at the mercy of the players of a Machiavellian politics. Even though there is a consensus against the mistake, there is no willingness to correct. As its evil consequence, there have been seven prime ministers during the short term of just five years. A crisis of confidence is rampant, and the superior values of society are at stake. In such a perplexing situation, people fail to understand the strength of the sovereignty vested in them through the written words of the constitution. This kind of situation is dangerous even for big and powerful countries. For a country like Nepal, which is in the vortex of a new type of cold war between two of its neighbours, it is difficult to reach a definite conclusion about whether the crisis is spontaneous or manipulated.

To learn more about the nature of conflict between India and China, a portion from a five-page report of the Intelligence Bureau as published in *The Statesman* is useful. It says:

> The Chinese militants have spread their area of operation in all the seven North-Eastern states and are running parallel administration with the help of local militants in the entire region, posing a serious threat to internal security.

There are various forms of war and Nepal has suffered the brunt of them in recent decades. As a landlocked country between two big military powers, Nepal has suffered a spate of economic blockades, sabotage of various types, and terrorism, all designed to bring the geo-strategically located Nepal, triggering the Indian security arrangements. Inciting people to engage in violence and rise up against the state, without declaring war, through propaganda is not new to Nepal. Whatever fosters traditional goodwill between the people of two countries is systematically being destroyed by unfounded and mischievous propaganda. Nepal is no match to counter such propaganda.

About a month ago, an Indian state minister for home affairs informed the Nepali parliament that India was aware of an arms consignment being delivered to terrorists in India by

Pakistan's secret service through Nepal. Neither the ruling party nor the opposition in Nepal took notice of the matter. This was not the first smuggling of its kind, nor would it be the last. This kind of propaganda gets space in newspapers not because they have space to fill. Indications are clear that Nepal has now become the target of propaganda on a par with that directed at Pakistan. It is logical to infer that by prejudicing the minds of average persons in India, there must be a certain design to be implemented against Nepal. Unknowingly, Nepal has been engulfed in the cold war-like situation between its neighbours. Indifference to the crisis may prove to be very costly to Nepal.

The historical peace which Nepal had enjoyed in the past from both of its neighbours vanished soon after China took military control over Tibet in 1950. Considering this move as a threat, India has been continuously attempting since then to involve Nepal in its security system. As this state is being forced through various overt and covert operations, Nepal has been under severe strain due to all-around instability and disorder. Besides awareness of contemporary events, several historical documents and memoirs testify that every measure, political change, upheaval and overthrow of the government has necessarily been a reflection of the conflict between Nepal's big neighbours. Both India and China have pursued their policies regarding Nepal irrespective of any consideration of a particular political system. They always give their national interests supreme consideration. None of the Communist movements in Nepal may be desirable for the national interests of China. And, similarly, even the self-declared pro-Indian democratic force in Nepal may not be in favour of the security interests of India. Communists can be a good camouflage for India's covert operations and, similarly, pro-Indian elements or persons of Indian origin may be a useful cover to promote the interests of China. This is not fully a hypothetical scenario. The support which the traditional institution of monarchy has from Communist China may not be there for the king of Bhutan and, similarly, a democratic India may not have the same level of support for the democratic forces of Bhutan which it has for the king of Bhutan. As both these powers are competing against each other around Nepal, always keeping their national interests supreme, it would not be realistic to assess only the internal reasons behind the perpetuating nature of political instability.

There is another dimension of the situation which is throttling the prospect for democratic systems in the whole region. Democratic and dictatorial regimes have different ways to prepare for defense and war. Too much militarisation adversely affects a democracy by making the army dominant. In the past, too much militarisation of Germany and Italy paved the way for dictatorship and, thus, destroyed their democracies. That trend ultimately resulted in World War II. With excessive militarisation of the United States of America during World War II, General Douglas MacArthur emerged as a force who was able to call for a repressive legislation to curb the influence of communism. Despite the legislation having had deterrent provisions, including capital punishment, the U.S. Supreme Court had to nullify those provisions to protect the freedoms of speech and expression. Again, there was the emergence of a war hero in power when President Eisenhower won unprecedented popular support. But again, there were deep-rooted democratic institutions in America to keep the power in the civil leadership. Based upon a rich tradition of European democratic practices, the American contribution to the matter of judicial review over legislation has always been a matter of inspiration for other democracies.

But the trend in South Asian countries is in a critical stage. Comparatively bigger countries in this area have inherited the kind of the army, intelligence and bureaucracy organised for the purpose of using them against their own people to protect colonial rule. Ideals of democracy and the supremacy of popular consent had never been in their ethos. The reservation of democracy is possible when the army, intelligence and bureaucracy are within the control of a popularly elected civil leadership. Unfortunately, two big countries in the region, India and Pakistan, born in animosity due to their partition, pay the price of hostility to each other. Because of its size and strength, India has always been considered to be a threat to the survival of Pakistan. The excess of militarization espoused to overcome this threat has always put Pakistan under one or another military ruler. An endangered Pakistan is forced to be in close alliance with China, which was already a threat to Indian security. This has put all three countries into a limitless race for arms and ammunition. Since a short duration war between India and China in 1962, India has entered into a phase of extraordinary militarisation. It is pathetic that, despite having the largest number of poor and illiterate people in the world, India has been the biggest buyer of arms and ammunition from the world market. Its consequences are found in politics. Whenever there is any serious difference between the army and the civil leadership, the decision of the army seems to prevail. Its perceptions of security supersede all other considerations. The security of the nation is the top priority in India and, therefore, its security agencies have the ultimate say.

India has expanded and diversified its secret services with respect to various aspects in target countries. According to a study conducted by journalist Salamat Ali a few years ago, India had about a dozen separately run intelligence agencies active in its neighbouring countries. These agencies not only collect information but also conduct various kinds of dirty tasks. The three wings of India's army and each state government have their own separate intelligence organisations operating in neighbouring countries. All are unknown to each other. The Research and Analysis Wing (RAW) is used mainly for political purposes. It is tasked to gather information and manipulate affairs in the industrial, commercial and banking sectors of other countries. Functioning in anonymity is their main trait. They are not visible anywhere, but the results of their performances are visible everywhere. Their dangerous missions have been used to train and export terrorists to neighbouring countries. Sri Lanka has been the worst case of their adventure, and its spillover caused the murder of even Rajiv Gandhi, India's promising leader. The fact that the policy of exporting terrorists and destabilising regimes has not been relaxed is an indication that it is beyond the reach of a popularly accountable civil leadership.

Civil leaders appeared to have been sidelined while vital decisions were made regarding the area of operation of its intelligence services. Even after Mrs. Indira Gandhi emerged as a strong leader, she deputed the RAW to deal with a charismatic politician of Nepal who had issued an ideological appeal for a revolution in his country. She was informed of an operation in Sikkim to merge it into India only a day earlier than it started. If the approval of a prime minister of her reputation was taken for granted, as was the case with Sikkim, one can easily guess how much the present prime minister, who has to depend upon a vacillating coalition of 13 political parties, might have been briefed about the operations conducted by the army, paramilitary and secret services,.

Soon after assuming the position of prime minister in his present term, Mr. Girija Prasad Koirala complained that a foreign power had played a role in Nepal in making and unmaking the government. It is a matter of record that Mrs. Indira Gandhi told him that her defeat was due to a conspiracy masterminded by Ramnath Kao, the RAW chief at that time. An investigation into the role of RAW in the murder of Mr. Rajiv Gandhi was also mysteriously concealed. There have also been allegations that the agency was misused to settle internal conflicts instead of confining its role to activities in neighbouring countries. The increasing role of the army and the secret services is more compatible with fascists like fundamentalists and religious fanatics who emphasise an expansionist design than with liberals who espouse social welfare and the rule of law. A great democracy in this region is in a serious stage of metamorphosis from a liberal democracy to an aggressive regional power. This is reminiscent of the phase through which Germany and Italy passed. At a crossroads, India carries the fate of the region between civil and military rule. Nepal cannot remain unaffected by this regional crisis.

Nepal has enough internal problems as a developing country trying to plant an alien concept of democracy in an adverse socio-economic background. But its external challenges are much more serious and may actually thwart all attempts at development and democracy. The coming years may prove to be fateful in determining whether or not these two ends can be had together. India has appeared as the epicentre in the process of destabilizing the regimes of the region. If all of the security apparatuses of India are brought within civil control through democratic procedures, democracy has a very bright prospect in this region. On the other hand, if security interests prevail overall, not only would democracy be lost but the whole region would also suffer devastation.

As far as the present crisis of Nepal is concerned, if there is no hostile treatment from its nearest neighbour, the people of Nepal have shown the character needed to create an ideal democracy. Democracy is not a switch-operated mechanism. It must be developed step-by-step, through practice. No modern art of governance can be learnt by the people or leaders without some mistakes being made in the process.

XII

Institutional and Legal Framework for Controlling Corruption

Nepali Perspective

Before entering into the subject matter—Nepal in the South Asian context—it is relevant to mention the findings of Berlin-based Transparency International. Among the least corrupt of countries, Singapore is ahead of Britain and the United States and Hong Kong are ahead of Germany and France. Brazil, the 49th least corrupt country is much ahead of India, the only South Asian country listed in the report.

It is also interesting to refer to a report published in a recent issue of *The Economist* regarding corruption control measures in Brazil, which has improved its records of democratisation and economic growth.

"Every one of those files in a scandal I am investigating", says a senior prosecutor in Brazil, waving his arm at the 97 fat folders on his shelves. In most cases, he expects to find evidence of public money going astray and to take the matter to the court. But based on the past performance, he expects that in half of them, he will win the court case but fail to recover the missing money or see the guilty jailed.

Probably no country in South Asia can claim even that extent of success in controlling corruption.

No country is immune to corruption. To keep corruption under control is a problem even in highly developed democracies. But that endeavour is much more complicated in the context of countries in what is known as the Third World. Developed countries are developed in terms of institutions of governance and have legal traditions to tackle corruption. Backed by highly industrialised economies and high rates of literacy, these countries have been able to keep the governance open, effective and accountable to those who are sovereign—the people. In developed nations, the system of accountability works automatically, and the leadership may play very little role in it. But in developing countries the status of the sovereign, the people, is precarious. As institutions in a transitional phase are fragile, the role of the leadership is a key factor to determining the success of the institutions. Singapore has a better record with respect to fighting corruption than even Britain and the United States mainly due to the role of its leadership. Other developing countries which lack a determined and capable leadership lie on the other extreme of the spectrum as the most corrupt. These include some countries of South Asia and countries like Nigeria.

All developing countries are not similar. As a unit, South Asia is the poorest area of the world. More than half of the world's illiterates and individuals below the poverty line live in South Asia. No country in South Asia is politically stable. Each country in this area feels seriously threatened by at least one neighbour across its border. It is common to find a powerful undercover operation attempt to destabilise the internal order of a neighbour. Age-old distrust, mistrust, and animosity keep them away from friendly dialogue and cooperation. In such a hostile external and internal environment, keeping governance open, accountable and effective is an uphill task, particularly for small countries. The problem of corruption is the net result of the total situation. Corruption thrives in a situation of political instability. In a developing stage, every country has loopholes in governance. No country in South Asia is in a position to get rid of this handicap independently.

Historically, the governance of the countries of this region developed along two distinct patterns. Countries once part of British India had a long apprenticeship in the British form of administration and legal system. Despite rampant poverty and illiteracy, these countries inherited the structures of administration and forms and procedures of the British democratic standard. They had lived under a guarantee of good governance but were denied self-governance. Leaders like Mahatma Gandhi were right, however, when they said that there couldn't be good governance without self-governance. The pressure of public opinion in all these countries after their independence has been to have both self-governance and good governance.

Nepal and Bhutan had different backgrounds of political development. Nepal, which has always been independent, has its own indigenously evolved institutions of governance. Since changing in 1951 from a feudal oligarchy to a democracy, Nepal has been experimenting through trial and error to find an appropriate form of governance The present constitution is the fifth one under trial. The instability generated by the great upheaval in 1990 has had multiplier effects in the country. This kind of situation is very vulnerable to anarchy and corruption. And Nepal has been suffering seriously from both.

The problem of corruption has to be seen in the totality of the situation. A cause-and-effect relationship has to be taken into account to deal with this problem. To have a motive of unlawful gain for oneself or others is an evil practice in governance. In Nepal, corruption has always been considered to be a serious crime against the state. King Prithvi Narayan Shah the Great, who unified modern Nepal in 1769, declared that even the death penalty would not be unjust to a person taking a bribe. It is evident that even the death penalty to an offender does not eliminate the vice. Many benevolent dictators of the past and present have failed to eliminate corruption even with such a harsh punishment. Democracy has its own strengths and weaknesses. Since 1951, Nepal has been experimenting with various forms of democratic governance having basic elements such as the separation of powers, representation and accountability. In the matter of controlling corruption, it has, till the present moment, had disappointing results despite the creation of a kind of public vigilance body. Since the broadening of the franchise for representation, politicians have been pressed into indulging in corrupt practices to come into power and, by all means, have power accessible to them. And it is difficult to guard the guard.

Keeping public opinion against corruption in mind, a Prevention of Abuse of Authority Commission was created in 1975 through the Third Amendment to the Constitution of Nepal. It had the power to investigate, prosecute and punish. All these powers were vested in one authority. Its rule had an overriding strength over the constitution. It used to initiate investigations even on its own initiative. In due course of time, it proved by its functions that it was a modem version of the

Star Chamber of medieval England. It victimized public servants using the pick-and-choose method. Many notorious offenders escaped from its watch, and credible persons denied the benefit of the doubt. In the case of the export of carpets, a prime minister of that time and several senior ministers, the governor of the central bank, and secretaries of several ministries were put on trial and the case ultimately turned into a fiasco during a political upheaval in the country. By studying the case impartially, one can conclude that the commission was used as an instrument of political vendetta. In the change of 1990, the commission was abrogated along with the constitution. But history seems to be repeating itself in a different manner.

The 1990 Constitution of the Kingdom of Nepal reintroduced this body as the Commission for the Investigation of Abuse of Authority (CIAA) and revised its role. In essence, the present constitution has given it mainly the role of a vigilance body accountable to Parliament. But the law enacted by Parliament has assigned it powers of the executive. Officials of the commission consider their power inadequate to punish offenders, whereas agencies of the government complain about its encroachment into the domain of the executive. The 1990 Constitution conferred upon the Attorney General the power to give the final consent to prosecute a crime against the state, and corruption is a crime against the state under the law of the country. The commission filed several cases without the final approval of the Attorney General that were, at the appeal stage, rejected by the Supreme Court. But the Supreme Court did not interpret the law clearly and has yet to clear up the confusion. It can hardly be presumed to have issued a pronouncement against the words and the spirit of the constitution.

In the meantime, the government, being pressured to take strong measures against corruption, has placed before Parliament three bills regarding the offence of and punishment for corruption, establishing a special tribunal to deal with such cases and an amendment to the law regarding the powers and functions of the CIAA. Till now, the law in Nepal has presumed the innocence of a person till the charge against him is proved beyond reasonable doubt. The element of motive had been necessary to establish guilt, but that condition will no longer be necessary after the promulgation of the new act.

With regard to the formation of the tribunal, the provisions of the constitution have been disregarded. The constitution guaranteed that people would be tried and punished only by regular courts, the justices of which were appointed by His Majesty the King on the recommendation of the Judicial Council. Guilty persons can be imprisoned up to ten years and their properties can be confiscated by a tribunal. Nepal is a signatory of several conventions on the civic and political rights of the people assuring that they will be tried by regular court judges and have several other such protections. A proposed amendment to the act regarding the CIAA also appears to be against the letter and the spirit of the constitution. A government that has given up its powers to discipline public servants lawfully has exceeded its limit in initiating bills with draconian effects.

If there is too much unrealistic and populist pressure upon the government to deal sternly with the problem of corruption, it will have adverse effects upon the liberty and initiative of the people. With the bill as it exists, no public servant will have the courage to bear the risk of making decisions and executing them fearlessly. In the past, under oligarchic rule, there had been very harsh laws that made the bureaucracy of Nepal introverted, timid and conspiratorial. That character was revived during the arbitrariness of the panchayat rule. Now, the same old wine is being put into a new bottle. Nepal is again going to be authoritarian in populist garb. The dreams of the people, the majority of whom are poor and illiterate, are again going to be disturbed by populists and power-mongers.

A country like Nepal must include among its several priorities the control of corruption. But doing so should not be at the cost of democratic ideals or the prospect of economic development. Too much stress upon repressive measures under the pretext of controlling corruption may introduce despotism from the back door. If it were possible to eliminate corruption by harsh punishment, this offence would not exist in dictatorial regimes.

There are genuine questions haunting the minds of common people. They wonder why they do not, as declared by the constitution, feel that they have sovereign power? What remedy do they have when their representatives in power abuse that power for personal greed and petty interests? Why do judges and officers fail in their obligations? How can their ballots be correctly reflected in the results? And how can the evil of corruption be controlled? The answers to all these questions are present in democracy. But democracy requires that people play their part, too. In the matter of corruption, the vigilance of the people has changed things in Nepal. For example, the special facility of members of Parliament and other high officials to import luxury vehicles came under serious criticism by the people. The press played its part effectively. Politicians apprehended the repercussions of their behaviour in the ensuing elections. And, thus, there was a change in the policy.

In our nascent democracy, there is a tendency to ignore the importance of public opinion. Finding no quick response, over-enthusiastic people resort to arms and violence in desperation. The results of such actions ultimately harm the people more than their inaction would have. Democracy provides a slow but stable remedy to all public grievances. Once the power of public opinion asserts itself, no authority in a democracy can persist for long in its unfair actions. Parliament is a supreme forum in which to vent the grievances of the people. To make Parliament more responsive to public interests, political parties have come into competition. To assist the people and Parliament, the CIAA can be of great use if it confines itself to its role as an authority accountable to Parliament. The constitution facilitates that act, but an act of Parliament has confused that provision. There is a need to remove this confusion and preserve the constitution.

Regarding the provision of information to the people and the formulation of public opinion, the World Bank, the sovereign of all sovereigns of the world, in its 1997 report suggests that the "availability of information helps citizens discipline public officials at the ballot box and through other avenues of protests, such as challenges and direct petitions to decision makers." It mentions some specific ways available to people living in a democratic state:

- In democracies, citizens can vote officials out of office if they believe them to be corrupt. This gives politicians an incentive to stay honest and work for the interests of their constituents.
- If courts are independent and citizens can sue to force the government to comply with the law, this opens another route to control government malfeasance.

- Public exposure of corruption through the media is another option. Even undemocratic rulers are likely to be sensitive to public opinion, if only because they wish to avoid being overthrown. A free press can be a vital check on abuses of power, especially in countries that lack other means of constraining politicians and bureaucrats.

There is a lurking fear in all fragile democracies that an unthoughtful movement against corruption may give corrupt elements the opportunity to do away with the democratic system with an illusory promise of good governance. Whatever measures are adopted, corruption is a menace with which the world, particularly the Third World, will have to live for a long time to come.

XIII

Comment on the Role of Leadership and Political Development

Because I was a man of a different professional discipline, a man with knowledge of the history and political development of Nepal, I initially felt inhibited about joining the debate. But perhaps studies in the social sciences are better examined with the knowledge of a layman. Shyam Bhurtel and Krishna Khanal have done a commendable job. They have been able to maintain adequate impartiality and objectivity in their analysis. Their basic premises can hardly be disputed. Their major thrust is the democratic aspect of political development. In my view, this thrust could be one of the several modernizing ideals of a developing society. In Nepal's context, I prefer to comment on one aspect of modernisation, that related to national identity. I believe nationalism is the most important ideal in the process of modernisation. It is on this point that I want to add my emphasis.

The independence of a nation, like the freedom of an individual, is a matter of constant vigilance, and any laxity costs both much. The freedom of an individual is very much conditioned by the independence of the country in which he or she resides; only in a free and stable nation can one hope for a better prospect of democratic modernisation. Developing countries that lack the inherent strength to survive lack the environment needed for the smooth functioning of the democratic institutions.

The authors of the paper have aptly remarked that the leadership role in developing societies is completely different from that in developed countries. And leadership in developing societies, in their view, cannot be confined to a business-like transactional role. They explain very convincingly how leaderships in the Third World have to play a transactional and a transformational role simultaneously.

The paper does not adequately discuss the variations in the development of institutions and infrastructures in Third World countries with different levels of development. This fact might have prompted them to refer to a "fourth world." I would, however, refrain from using this term while discussing certain peculiarities of small and developing countries such as Nepal.

Some countries with a colonial past have been able to share a great level of economic growth and development of political institutions despite the loss of the most valuable of things—national identity. In contrast, some countries, without having undergone the painful experience of colonial rule, have had to introduce the process of all-round development virtually from the scratch. This distinction has a marked effect on the leadership and the political development of such countries. Countries with a large area, large populations and many resources, including expansive coastal access, are much better off in every sense than countries sandwiched between big and unpredictable neighbours. With the advent of a modern form of government, countries without a colonial past, countries which have primitive and traditional socio-economic conditions, have been confronted with the big and powerful adversaries in the global as well as regional levels. Besides other hegemonic interests, these small and poor countries, despite their rich cultural heritages, are unable to deal with the powerful shocks and impacts of the machination and propaganda of bigger countries. In the free trade of ideas and institutions, small and poor countries are always at the receiving end.

There has been great politicisation in all Third World countries, but the propelling issues have been very different for each. Countries under colonial subjugation had a nationalistic urge as the main thrust of mass consciousness. That urge, however, was not as strongly present in independent countries, where the masses have instead been aroused with vague sentimental issues. The masses have never responded enthusiastically to the modern concept of democracy in any traditional society. In general people have been apathetic towards any kind of popular leadership with modernising ideals as goals. Because of the basic human instinct of territorial attachment, feelings of nationalism are very easily generated. Nationalism was the main issue through which several charismatic leaders of the Third World rose to power. Whether it was Mahatma Gandhi, Ho Chi Minh, Sukarno or Jawaharlal Nehru—these leaders were the product of great nationalistic struggles. Countries which did not experience colonial rule had traditional leaders. In countries lacking powerful emotional issues to motivate and galvanise the masses, leadership with a mere democratic ideal has a hard time emerging. It is in this context that the role of the traditional institution in both transactional as well as transformational roles can be stressed.

The concept of nationalism in an independent but traditional society is related to the stability of the powers that be and because of vested interests in perpetuating one's hold over the power, whosoever is in the seat of power becomes the champion of the stability of the nation. Unfortunately, rivals and competitors for power have a tendency either to raise divisive and parochial issues based upon ethnicity, race and language to organise the people or seek foreign patronage. Nationalism is a modern phenomenon in these countries. Before the urge for nationalism can be embedded in the conscious sentiments of people, traditional societies are confronted with the hazardous task of preserving their own independence. Ideals of democracy become meaningful when these are infused with adequate nationalistic spirit. When these two interests collide, the result is either authoritarian rule or loss of independence. Leadership has to prove its worth in such a precarious situation.

Internal forces are not the sole determining political elements in any independent country. The influence of external elements are found everywhere. But in case of the traditional societies, particularly small traditional countries, they are a major determinant. Big and powerful countries, even those with Third-World status, have a tendency to continually overpower and dictate the terms of affairs in smaller and poorer countries. Besides adopting the techniques of past colonial powers, large, powerful countries also engage in political machinations in order to control the minds and attitudes of the people of small countries. Instead of using armies, powerful countries help foment dissatisfaction to organise local proxy forces that can the coerce a government into accepting concessions. Knowingly or unknowingly, the politicians of small countries fall into such traps and, thus, lose not only their rights but also their identity as a free nation.

The learned authors have presented a correct perspective on the emergence of nationalism in Nepal. Its growth, as they say, cannot be equated with European nationalism or the nationalism of the "new states", which developed their sense of nationalism through a bitter and protracted struggle against alien rule. Nepal has its own historical background to the development of nationalism. The unification of Nepal was, certainly, an act of war and aggression, but it was not the sole reason for the emergence of Nepal as a nation. It had certain common religious and cultural components to unite it as a nation under the rule of a Hindu king who was—theoretically—supposed to rule according to the precepts laid down by the *Dharmasastras*. Because of these religious principles, the institution of the monarchy was able to integrate this multi-ethnic, multi-racial and multi-lingual society into one nation. As a great nation-builder, King Prithvi Narayan Shah was able to perceive the geo-political compulsions of this country. What he said about Nepal's being a yam between two boulders is still valid. Every major political event of this country has reflected this fundamental constraint. It is, therefore, inaccurate to analyse political events in Nepal without taking into account the role played by external forces.

The political instability caused by the decline and fall of the Moghul empire in India was an opportunity to unify the kingdoms of Nepal. Similarly, the prolonged stability in India under British rule favoured Nepal's consolidation. The interest of persons in power pushed Nepalis into formulating the most suitable strategies for survival between two unpredictable giants of the region. The presence of the British empire in India had a considerable influence on the political development of Nepal. British residents and emissaries have always been involved in power struggles and power games in the country. They were played not only by kings and their prime ministers but also by *bharadars* and strongmen, all pitting one against the other. There were always one or the other kinds of rebels, dissenters and enemies of the regime patronised and sheltered in India to overthrow the people in power. To trace the background of the involvement of external forces in the affairs of Nepal, I have referred to these facts of history, which speak for themselves.

The third part of the paper precisely analyses the facts and trends of a decade—1951 to 1960—with the Revolution of 1951 as the watershed event of the period.

The Revolution of 1951 was neither a one-act event nor an act of homogenous interests. The king wanted to restore his lost prerogative with the help of popular forces. Popular forces, under the banner of a party, wanted to seize power to introduce a democratic form of government. India was interested in having a manageable government to withstand the new challenge from the north. It was the culmination of all these interests which accomplished the change of 1951 and rendered it an odd compromise. The chronology of the fast-changing events of this region prove that the timing and method of the revolution were not internally determined and, therefore, that its beneficiaries were also not solely internal. About the method adopted in the revolution, I have an episode I would like to share with you. This episode was told to me by B.P. Koirala.

Soon after Prime Minister Mohan Shumsher released Mr. Koirala, he had talks with Jawaharlal Nehru on the future course he would follow. Mr. Koirala told Mr. Nehru that he was looking into the prospects of a Gandhi-type agitation. Mr. Koirala told me that he was dumbfounded when the avowedly Gandhian Nehru exploded with these words, "What nonsense is this Gandhism? Will the Ranas understand it?" This was the outburst of a person who was very soon going to extend to Mohan Shumsher a red-carpet welcome with a 21-gun salute. And, hoping to maintain stability for his regime, Mohan Shumsher conceded several provisions in the treaty to which otherwise he would have never agreed.

The authors are silent on the paradox of how revolutionaries were successful without much training or sacrifice. And, as the writers concede, for the cause of revolution, the revolutionaries had neither sought nor received popular participation. In spite of all these lacunas, the revolution terminated the Rana regime. The authors have curtly remarked that the heterogeneous alliance became activated and successful as it received the support of the king and the Indian government. This support determined the course of the revolution. As remarked by Leo Rose in his book, *Nepal: Strategy for Survival*, "struggle had not been fought in the hills of Nepal but in the halls of New Delhi where the Indian insistence upon the 'middle way' solution had dominated proceedings." Without minimizing the role played by various political leaders, in *Democratic Innovations in Nepal* Joshi and Rose again remarked that the revolution was fought between the Ranas and the Indian government in Delhi. Any serious study of that event leads to the same conclusion. There was, therefore, negotiation between unequals without any chance of meeting at one table. That sad truth of the revolution has its own grim lessons.

The change of 1951, however, was no ordinary event. It revolutionised the political process. Democratic values and ideals became the guiding principles of state policies. The hereditary rule of the Rana prime ministers was replaced by a popular and representative form of government. Monarchy acquired a new political legitimacy based upon the popular will in accordance with a modern democratic spirit.

But the aftermath of the revolution introduced great instability and uncertainty. There were no political institutions to cope with the great change. In the process of transferring and allocating power, no one had firm control over the situation. As a result, foreign involvement in the internal affairs of Nepal increased tremendously. Internal disputes were referred to foreign mediators, a procedure which helped a foreign diplomat emerge as the most powerful person in Nepal. Resigning from the government following a mysterious student agitation, B.P. Koirala on one occasion had to allege that the ambassador of India in Nepal was acting like the chairman of the district board of Muzaffarpur. As documented by Kusum Shrestha in *Monarchy in Nepal*, the Indian ambassador, in his address to workers and students of the ruling Nepali Congress party, even incited them against the home minister. I have verified knowledge of the exact utterance of the ambassador: "It is a matter of shame for you. If you can remove persons as powerful as the Ranas, why can't you remove this Koirala?"

During the decade of 1951–60, the political situation of Nepal reflects the instability that occurred due to the determinants of the change in 1951. This conflict continued even during the period of the parliamentary form of government. The first elected parliament was a great experiment in a modern form of government in Nepal for which adequate prerequisites were almost non-existent. The civil service, judiciary, press and other such institutions were all in formative stages. At the same time, rivalries among big powers all trying to spread their influence through various types of propaganda and ideological means had increased, and political parties were vulnerable to these influences. Relations between the two great neighbours of this country had deteriorated to the point of armed conflict. There were several reflections of this deterioration in Nepal's politics. The events which led to the abrogation of the parliamentary form of government are still shrouded in mystery. But the polarisation effect, which often cancels able ideologies, was no less responsible for it than other factors. Had the king not acted, some other force would have superseded him. The politics of Nepal was the concern of several international forces and this event was, therefore, not a consequence of the conflict among internal forces alone. Even a confirmed democrat like Nehru later revealed to a prominent Nepali minister that he had suggested to the king to do what he liked if he was not satisfied with Mr. Koirala. The king's anger was enflamed by the dissolution of the parliament as he was not sure he could manage whoever was chosen successor to Mr. Koirala. Facts about how Nehru managed to see people he trusted installed in the new political set-up have yet to become public. A conflict of international magnitude, thus, entered into a new phase of the panchayat system. The story of the panchayat system is the record of events characterised by conflict. In a new polity of consensus, the polarisation of forces into different parties and their ideological stands was not possible; thus, external arrangements were at odds in the struggle to build up permanently loyal groups and lobbies in the forums of the panchayat. The game of musical chairs for power was, on the one hand, a great corruptor of political characters and, on the other, a great destroyer of lobbies and groups loyal to external forces. This contradictory situation in the panchayat system hindered its development as a consensual system.

There have been several positive developments in this system, too. As local self-government units, villages, towns and district panchayats have been a great success. With the help of laws, people at the grassroots level have learnt to administer on a democratic basis. On the national level too, the legislature has followed various procedures which are familiar in several democracies. I am not suggesting that perfect democracy is found in the present system. But there can be no denial of the fact that, except for the legal recognition of political parties, the present constitutional order has imbibed the major essence of democracy and that that essence can be developed by the positive responses of the people. Mere legal documents do not create democracies; building a democratic system requires, naturally, a great deal of patience and tolerance. The most liberal constitution Germany had yet adopted paved the way for Nazis to move into power and a Fascist constitution did not prevent democrats from capturing power in Spain. A constitution is not a static document and I see enormous scope for further democratisation under the present constitution. By practice and through various decisions of the Supreme Court of the country, there have been some developments of the modern constitutional law. The freedoms of the individual have been defined and elaborated. Ours is a pluralistic society permitting the right to dissent, excepting the right to form political parties. A dictatorship inherent in a one-party system cannot function under such pluralism. The institution of the monarchy is a safeguard against any form of totalitarianism as it cannot go along with an all-powerful politburo and its secretary general at the top. The failure of the Back-to-the-Village National Campaign was thus natural.

In the paper, the learned authors mention the debate over the active and supreme leadership of the Crown. Whatever interpretations politicians might offer, the constitution has a clear provision in this regard. As legal sovereignty is vested in the king, he is the supreme body in the constitutional setup. He has the power to issue periodic directives to the executive in the interests of the country and the Nepali people. This is one very clear instance of the leadership of the king as laid down in the constitution. There has been a debate in India regarding the role of the president in the Indian constitution; at issue is whether or not the president is bound by the advice of the prime minister. Various jurists assert that the president of India has an active as well as assertive role to play. This cannot be any less in a monarchical system of democracy. Besides several provisions regarding his approving or disapproving ministerial acts and legislative bills, the king has certain inherent prerogatives in the form of residuary powers. Wherever there is power, it is presumed that it will be exercised in a bonafide fashion, and, in the matter of the exercise of royal prerogatives, the constitution has clear guidelines.

The debate regarding an "extra-constitutional underground gang of neo-courtiers" constituting the most powerful corridor of power with accountability to none is a very controversial topic indeed. Indeed, any comment on it would appear partisan. This allegation is so vague that there is no allegation to counter it. And, I am not going to argue as an amicus curiae on it. But I must say that lobbies and groups have been patronised by several external forces inside as well as outside the panchayat polity, and this allegation is an expression of one such force against the other. Every forum of politics, whether within the panchayat or outside, has been engulfed by personality clashes and group rivalries, not representing real people, but patrons—seen or unseen. The catchword "underground gang" now has been directed mainly against the power centre with the clear purpose of destabilising the present power structure. Anyone out of power may use it to foment popular discontent, and it does not come as a surprise if a person in power today shouts the same slogan tomorrow. The saddle of power makes a great difference in political views, and this difference is very much present in the panchayat. A person feels a sense of responsibility while in power, but with a loss of power, such responsibility also has a tendency to go away. A very serious challenge to the panchayat system is its inability to enroll and galvanise persons with sincere zeal and conviction. This is a typical Third-World case in the struggle for power, but it has been aggravated in Nepal because of its external contacts if the statement of Man Mohan Adhikari recorded in the book *Nepal: Year of Decision* is correct. As a great admirer of the Soviet strategies in this region, Mr. Adhikari has yet to enlighten us for whom and under which strategy the Soviet Union was bargaining for a lion's share in the leadership of the Back-to-the-Village National Campaign in 1976. I am circumscribed by time and space to give illustrations of other lobbies which are known to all. There have always been accommodations of persons in the power structure to balance one against the other of the externally patronised lobbies. This has increased opportunistic and unpredictable political leadership. There have been comments regarding the extraneous leanings of the prime ministers and ministers who come to power with great fanfare but are unceremoniously removed. It is relevant to quote from *Nepal: Profile of a Himalayan Kingdom* by Leo E. Rose and John T. Scholz:

> It is a normal phenomenon for the foreign policy of any society to be strongly affected by the domestic political and economic factors, and that is certainly the case in Nepal. But the reverse principle, namely, the international factors have a strong and decisive impact on Kathmandu's domestic policies—is even more apparent. This is a painful fact of life for many Nepalis, and one that some of them would prefer to ignore.

The writers of the paper have analysed the developments leading to the royal proclamation for the national referendum. I do not agree with the view that the student agitation of April 1979 was a challenge posed by anti-panchayat students. It is now an established fact that several prominent *panchas* were involved in inciting students to anarchic agitation and that a well-known critic of the panchayat system, B.P. Koirala, condemned that agitation. It was on this point that Mr. Koirala threatened to part company with his colleagues and friends in his party. He had returned home from exile apprehensive about the massive turmoil in the region, including in Nepal, and, for this view, had been expelled from his party. By his own experience, too, he was, therefore, very clear about the destabilising role of some foreign powers. Students were mere a proxy for them. Knowledgeable people have not yet revealed what transpired at midnight on 24 May, 1979, which resulted in the announcement of the referendum with the dawn of the day. Subsequent changes brought a new prime minister who, soon after, turned out to be a vociferous opponent of the "underground gang of neo-courtiers." And he was quite successful in pacifying all kinds of agitation and leading all forces of the panchayat to success in the referendum. The authors do not explain what role the "underground gang of neo-courtiers" or the then-prime minister played during the period. B.P. Koirala, who had returned home from exile to initiate a national consensus of broad spectrum, was compelled to lead a confrontation in the referendum, which he had accepted as a democratic exercise without bothering much which side won. With national consensus as his paramount goal, he accepted the verdict of the referendum, even though the process of democratisation was to him "heartbreakingly slow."

As a matter of fact, there was not a single complaint against the panchayat system in the charter of demands of the students. The referendum, however, brought a great change in the legitimacy as well as the structure of the panchayat system. As a consequence of the referendum, a new election system and method of nominating the prime minister were introduced. Both changes made the Rashtriya Panchayat more powerful. Elections have assumed importance in the political process and therefore have become costly and competitive. Elected offices are now beyond the reach of common people. Elections following the third amendment to the constitution have shown a trend that elections are being contested successfully either by the misuse of government funds or with enormous amounts of money supplied by foreign sources. One can easily judge, with common sense, the source of money depending on how a leader performs when elected. A determined group of subverters in an enlarged franchise can be used to make all democratic exercises futile. Considering this dangerous trend, it seems that it was too early to change the electoral method. It is doubtful in the present context to presume that a broadening of participation in politics by the people can "enhance the control of the government by the people." People are too ignorant, too poor and too traditional in their attitude to exercise their controlling power over the government. It is on this point of both experimenting with democracy and preserving stability that the role of the leadership assumes both transactional and transformational dimensions. In Nepal, the monarchy is the only institution which can provide active leadership in this transitional period.

Before I conclude, let me say a few words on the question of political parties. A political culture of pre-emptory as well as peremptory command, as defined by Rishikesh Shaha, has a predominant effect on the political development of the country. Whatever mode of ideals they pronounce, political parties in Nepal are not free from traditional political culture. Parties with democratic declarations have very little democracy inside them, and parties with equalitarian slogans are most unequal within their parties. A great deal of political literature has been distributed in the name of various political parties, but parties have always been careful not to circulate party rules containing the rights and duties of office bearers and general cadres. None of the leaders of any party has ever empowered delegates of the party to elect any office bearers, including the central leadership. Henry Maine's theory of the status to contract operates very well in the organisational set-up of these parties. These leaders have a genuine fear that their party might be subverted if delegates were permitted to elect office bearers. But they do not adopt the same outlook while demanding a share in the state power. Leaders who do not trust their own bonafide cadres in the matter of electing leadership and deciding the policies of the party have very little moral appeal while demanding a share in the state power on the basis of their parties. None of the leaders bother to consult any organ of the party before taking decisions or issuing statements of vital political importance. None of these parties have bothered to become a cadre-based party. In fact, political parties have not yet come out beyond a conceptual level. Soon after the Revolution of 1951, parties entered into the race for power and these power-oriented organizations are built on a "patron-client" relationship. Parties are not yet free from that attitude. In my opinion, there is no well-knit, democratically organised party in Nepal. With little accountability to their cadres or to the people in general, parties, on various occasions, on the whims and vagaries of their leaders, have become instruments for destabilisation in the hands of extraneous elements. Saying so is not a matter of denouncing the sincere endeavours of innumerable idealists who rendered everything of their lives to make the concept of party a reality. It is a matter of sincere heart-searching in the prevailing political situation.

The problem with the leaders of the multiparty side is that they have not been able to participate in the government for a long time. Detention, exile, persecution and sufferings have hardened their attitudes. Even in developed countries, when the opposition party remains out of power for a long time, it becomes anarchic and agitational. In Nepal, politicians of that kind are no exception. B.P. Koirala mentioned in his last days of life that his colleagues should have practiced some restraint and resilience. But he was the lone voice of conscience among all of the oppositional politics in Nepal. It cannot be denied that the common people have long had for a liberal democratic system . It is not a question of having a party of one's liking; it is a question related to the freedoms of conscience and expression, which includes the right to dissent, too. Any system which protects and promotes that freedom has an element of democracy. Sometimes, parties also curtail such freedoms. Thus, after the United States of America achieved independence, the federalists debated how not to allow parties to come into existence in their democracy. In Nepal at the present juncture, we have reached a point at which the role of political parties should not be mixed up with other democratic rights. Despite the flexibility of the constitution in the beginning, the panchayat system had a repressive and unpopular image.

After having made adjustments and accommodations with hard realities and several adverse elements of the country, the panchayat system has generally improved its image. It is again at the crossroads of being moulded into a one-idea authoritarian system or being developed into a partyless but pluralistic system. The imposition of an ideology goes against the basic tenets of democracy and the parameters of partylessness have to be enlarged to accommodate various shades of ideas and ideologies into its fold. With adequate patience and tolerance, partylessness can be made a meeting point of several democratic and modernising ideals. But in the absence of a national consensus, taking into view the threats and challenges the nation faces, no system of government and no form of democracy has a chance. If permitted to go into detail, one can prove that the panchayat system is the worst; but, in the present context, in my view, there is no better alternative to it. I fully share the view expressed by the writers that it was imperative for the transformational leadership to act as a "coalition-maker" for the broader political integration of the country. But that is not enough. As B.P. Koirala said on his deathbed, the opposition in the Third World has to be more responsible than the person in power. It is in the vital interest of the people that there be a national consensus based upon democratic norms to cooperate and, if possible, to participate in the concerted effort for economic growth and political institution-building. Impulsive reactions to the vulgar utterances of lightweight persons of any political leaning must not provoke the statesmen and politicians of a country. Above all these things, there should be awareness that the independence of a country is a pre-condition for individual liberty; our struggle for liberty should not jeopardise national independence. But in a typically underdeveloped country, such a show of wisdom from the opposition is rare.

(This commentary was prepared in December 1986)

XIV

The Nation's Right

The Constitution of the Kingdom of Nepal is a synthesis: it not only guarantees the rights of individuals but also safeguards the vital interests of the nation, thus infusing democracy with nationalism. The petition filed by Bal Krishna Neupane involved both the issue of both individual freedom as well as national interest. What the Supreme Court decided is that not only does a petitioner have the right to be informed of the functions of the state and seek a remedy in any matter concerning the public interest but also that concerning treaties of any nomenclature, including ones concerning the sharing of natural resources, require ratification by Parliament.

Complete Failure

The nation is, without doubt, in complete agreement with the prime minister when he says that water resources hold the key to the success of Nepal's development. Unfortunately, however, completely failed to take the nation into confidence regarding the agreement he reached with India on water resources. In fact, at the time he declared he would do one thing but under the mechanism of unseen hands, the result turned out entirely different, tarnishing his own image and prestige.

In the past, Nepal has had bitter experiences with India on river water agreements. Even a scholar like S.D. Muni who frequently casts aspersions on Nepal's national sentiments, in his recent book, *India and Nepal,* admits that there is "some truth in the allegation of one sided and exploitative use of Nepali water resources by India in what is known as mutual benefit projects between the two countries such as Koshi and Gandak projects." B.G. Verghese, in his book *Waters of Hope,* explains: "India speaks as an upper riparian when it addresses Bangladesh and turns the argument when it talks to Nepal." Jagat Mehta, India's former foreign secretary, is remembered for his generous view towards Nepal on water resources in his writing the *Failure of Diplomacy.* Muchkund Dubey, India's former foreign secretary, told a recent seminar that Nepal wanted merely 25 megawatts from the Tanakpur Barrage. Clearly, Nepal can muster the support of a large number of conscientious people in India if those people are properly informed. We have not been able to tap into this tremendous amount of goodwill in India towards Nepal.

Prime Minister Girija Prasad Koirala faced tough negotiations with India on the Transit Treaty as New Delhi wanted to review the whole gamut of relations from the Indian point of view. Koirala's opposition to the former regime in Nepal is well known; he even went to the extent of asking India not to budge from its stand, implying political conditions. However, when he visited India as prime minister in 1991, he quickly realized that India had no permanent friend in Nepal but only her permanent national interest. The talks almost failed. Indeed, it was only after a one-to-one meeting between

Koirala, who had no experience or proven ability in diplomacy, and P.V. Narasimha Rao, with a long history of diplomatic experience and proven diplomatic skills, that a miracle happened. It took a year-long constitutional battle to find out the suppressed text of the "miracle" in the form of the virtual surrender of Nepal's national interests to India. A treaty in the form of an Agreed Minutes was implemented secretly while the text of the recommendation of the inter-governmental task force was published in Nepal Gazette without head or tail to escape the rigours of ratification by Parliament. An entire year passed by debating whether the document was a treaty or an understanding.

Details regarding Nepal's other rivers are conspicuous by their absence in the Agreed Minutes. Even the recommendations of the task force are cleverly worded. For example, it refers to handing over financing and investments regarding some river projects to India though Nepal's stand has been for the equitable sharing of investments and benefits. Giving up her riparian rights, Nepal also did not raise objections to India's unilateral construction of the Tanakpur Barrage.

Thus, Nepal made available land and natural resources contained within its boundaries for the completion of the Tanakpur structures without asserting the right to the equitable sharing of the barrage's benefits. By relinquishing this right, Nepal had to humiliatingly accept an insignificant quantity of water and power. The modalities of getting even these few benefits are subject to negotiations.

Water resource experts fear the severe degradation of the environment following the planned diversion of the Mahakali River and its tributaries to India with the help of the afflux bund on Nepal's high ground. The area occupied by the left afflux bund is more than the 2.9 hectare claimed by the government. But even more problematic is that it is not very clear how much of Nepal's territory will be submerged when the barrage becomes fully operational. Some estimate that as many as 3,000 hectares of land will be affected.

Riparian Right

The Tanakpur Agreement definitely grants India permanent use of Nepal's land and resources. It undermines Nepal's right as a riparian state. This may even have harmful implications in the future while defending our rights to our other natural resources.

India quite possibly used the Transit Treaty as leverage to dictate to Mr. Koirala the terms of the water accords. In order to evade democratic scrutiny and confuse the general public, the accord was described as an "understanding." It is a widely accepted principle of international law that a treaty signed under fraudulent circumstances and coercion is void. In practice, given Nepal's size, the ground reality could be different.

Legally and practically, the Mahakali River is the boundary river between Nepal and India up to the Tanakpur Barrage. The left afflux bund is an integral part of the barrage. According to Oppenheim, a classic authority in international law: "If a river lies wholly, that is, from its source to its mouth within the boundary of one and the same state, that is known as the national river." Mahakali, thus, is not a national river. In 1920, Nepal agreed to transfer territory to India in exchange for the land on which Sarada Barrage was constructed. Though the barrage was fully inside Indian territory, British rulers in India exhibited a sense of justice and equity towards Nepal by conceding water for irrigation as a right. The Tanakpur Barrage is, in fact, an alternative to the Sarada Barrage, which has outlived its engineering life. However, the right acknowledged by the British has not been recognised in the Tanakpur Barrage agreement which extends into Nepal.

Obsolete Theory

An obsolete theory of absolute sovereignty, known as the Harmon Doctrine, has been enforced to deny riparian rights to Nepal. The Mahakali is a boundary river up to the Tanakpur Barrage. As such, Nepal has the right of lower riparian. India has been claiming the right of lower riparian in almost all rivers in Nepal, but the same claim is being denied to Nepal with respect to the Mahakali River. To India, rivers from Nepal are "common" whereas those to Bangladesh are not.

Our state-run media, which lacks credibility, recently gave much publicity to a comment by A.G. Noorani, a Bombay-based lawyer, who questioned the validity of the Supreme Court verdict on the Tanakpur case. Coming from a citizen of a country which continues to fight to preserve territory where "not even a single blade of grass grows," he has a different approach toward Nepal's territory. He says: "Some areas are likely to be submerged on the Nepali side, but this land is a riverbed only."

M.P. Jain, a noted authority on Indian constitutional law, says in the context of the concept of the continental shelf: "The framers of the constitution had taken the view that anything above the land goes with the land. If there is a tree above the land, the tree goes with the land. Water is above the land and so it goes with the land." It can thus be argued that the water of the Mahakali has submerged land in Nepal and that the water goes with the land. Under the Helsinki rules on water sharing, Nepal, as the basin state of the Mahakali, has a right.

As long as Nepal remains an open society and a pluralistic democracy, national sentiments will continue to be forcefully expressed and the national interest vigorously defended. Any threat to wipe out political forces defending the national interest or even attempting to amend constitutional safeguards would only be counterproductive. What Nepal needs with regard to the Tanakpur Barrage is not a charitable gift but a national right.

(This commentary was first published in The Independent Weekly, 20 January 1993)

XV

Nepal, India and China:
A Triangular Relationship on Trial

It is sometimes said that the foreign policy of Nepal is too politicised. This happens when there is a lack, or disregard, of national consensus. Besides, whenever people perceive that their national interest is becoming unsafe, there is a natural instinct of self-preservation which stimulates them to express themselves politically. After all, eternal vigilance is required not only for the liberty of an individual but also for the independence of a nation, too.

There rarely is an instance elsewhere of a small country like Nepal, landlocked between two of the most populous and biggest countries of the world, having very different traditions, having survived with uninterrupted independence since the recorded history of mankind. Nepal has a unique advantage from its geographical situation: any attempt of one neighbor to subjugate it invites the other to retaliate. It is between the soft bellies of security of two powerful nations, and equidistance has been proved as the best policy for Nepal. Whenever Nepal has deviated from such a policy, reprisals seem to be coming from the affected side. The designs by one to prevail in Nepal have always been countered by the other. This geo-political compulsion to maintain equidistance is sometimes misunderstood. China's finger-and-palm view considers Nepal as one of its fingers. Similarly, there is an Indian view which considers the Himalayas as a common security line. But these views have proved to be irrelevant.

It is an established fact that Nepal is in a politically seismic zone as its two neighbours have the tendency to conflict. After India's independence in 1947 and China's liberation in 1949, there was a great political convergence in Nepal in 1951. Following that event, it was declared that political power would remain under popular control through democratic institutions. Undergoing several political experiments, Nepal again has a multiparty democracy and a constitutional monarchy. During these changes, there have been many reflections of the uneasy relations between Nepal's two neighbours.

One has to remember Prof. Leo Rose, who once said that "international factors have a strong and often decisive impact on Kathmandu's domestic policies."

Nepal's relations with her two neighbours have passed through several tests of time, especially in recent decades. Jawaharlal Nehru, as a scholar, had a strong knowledge of Nepal's close relation with China. But as a prime minister, he had been warned and repudiated by two successive regimes in China when he claimed that Nepal fell within the security line of India. Kaisher Bahadur K.C., who was assigned as a diplomat, has revealed information about Nehru's talks with both Chiang Kai-shek during the Kuomintang rule and Mao Zedong during the Communist rule. Again, what Nehru said in 1960—that an aggression on Nepal would be considered as an aggression on China herself—was repeated by Chen Yi in

1962. With treaties or without treaties, each of our neighbours has expressed its concerns whenever its interests were affected by the overtures of the other.

Nehru's statement in 1960 sparked off, for the very first time, a very serious controversy about the treaty of 1950. Later Nehru accepted the interpretation given by B.P. Koirala: that India could help Nepal only at its request and not unilaterally. It was obvious to all that the 1950 treaty was procured under the coercion of insurgency. Such a treaty does not command respect in international law. This treaty was incomplete as it was neither ratified nor implemented. Thus, it remained disused. A law which remains disused for a long time does not have much effect. After the democratic changes in Nepal in 1951, various unilateral, bilateral and multi-lateral commitments have been made, modifying Nepal's relations with her neighbours. In the context of the 1950 treaty, a letter of exchange was also signed on the same date under the same signatories. In it, the government of India recognized the necessity of protecting Nepali nationals from unrestricted competition. This need was further explained by Nehru in 1952 and then by Foreign Minister Dinesh Singh in 1966. Such unilateral declarations, under the Ihlen Doctrine of international law, work in favour of Nepal .

A treaty with legal validity has to be interpreted in a just and fair way. Self-preservation is the supreme natural right of a nation and no treaty can be interpreted against this principle. Nepal cannot survive as a nation if its door is swung open in an unrestricted manner to the nationals of a country with a population 40 times bigger than Nepal's. During British rule in India, not even British nationals, let alone Indians were allowed to visit Nepal or buy immovable property without prior permission, whereas Nepalis were permitted to go to

India without restriction and buy property, even in Britain. The sense of justice in the imperial power is painfully lacking in independent and democratic India.

Access to the sea is key to Nepal's prosperity, but, again, the leaders of independent India failed to maintain the concession given by the imperialist power which ruled India. In 1923, the British rulers in India concluded a treaty which provided a permanent transit right to Nepal. But this was withdrawn in 1950, and now a periodically negotiable treaty always compels Nepal to surrender its vital interests as a nation. The high expectations of the people were betrayed after the restoration of multiparty democracy in Nepal, for which there was great support in India, too. Nepal was given a temporary facility of transit and, in return, an inexperienced and highly obliged prime minister of Nepal was asked to rubber stamp a policy the astute bureaucrats of India had already decided. Furthermore, concepts such as harnessing Nepal's rivers as common rivers and permitting Indian nationals to compete in various jobs and opportunities in Nepal, to name a few, were secretly agreed upon. This fact is now surfacing in unofficial sources in India. The Constitution of Nepal guarantees the people of Nepal one more fundamental right: the right to be informed. It took one year's struggle in the Supreme Court to find out how much Nepal had lost in the Tanakpur Barrage Treaty.

Refugees coming from Bhutan have emerged as yet another very serious problem between Nepal and India. India should have been the main party for resolving the problem but India is diverting Butanese refugees to Nepal. India has a treaty obligation with Bhutan to treat the Bhutanese as nationals in India but is not allowing them to stay in India or contributing on humanitarian grounds. People in Nepal know the purpose behind "the Greater Nepal" propaganda, but they do not have the leadership to communicate their grievances to the Indian government. As a culmination of all these bitter experiences, whenever people grumble, it is branded as anti-Indian feeling. To the new leadership in power, nationalism is not a favourite subject. Even the architects and beneficiaries of the foreign policy of the previous order as ministers and secretaries were waiting for an opportunity to denounce nationalism as an "anti-Indian" policy. But that condemnation has not silenced the people in building up a powerful opinion in favour of national interests and nationalism. Nepal has a prime minister who consoles India, saying that there is "anti-Indian" element in Nepal. Actually, he has failed to represent Nepali nationalism. Recent experience in Nepal suggests that a person who does not like to represent national interests not only loses his political image but also tarnishes the image of a friendly country too. The sense of Nepali nationalism has never been so hurt and goodwill towards India has never been at such a low ebb. It would be a gross mistake to minimise this popular sentiment as mere instigation.

No one is accusing India of being anti-Nepali in spite of several instances of unjust treatment. People in India were made to believe that Nepal has a "Greater Nepal" design. It was an excuse to drive out persons of Nepali origin, not only from India but also from Bhutan. The process started in the northeastern states of India and Bhutan followed the "guidance" and active support of the Indian security agencies. Similarly, there were a large number of terrorist camps in India acting against Nepal. This fact came to light during a court trial in Nepal. Nepalis are familiar with the threat of the Sri Lankan case repeating in Nepal. Such activities do not help to promote traditional good neighbourly relations. The urge to foster good relations compels us to spell out where we are failing. Even quite recently, a threat of violence was issued from a terrorist camp in India, obviously in reaction to the private visit of the prime minister to Tibet, where he was suspected to have taken part in high-level talks behind India's back.

The greatest hurdle to maintaining normal relations is the lack of communication. China and the Chinese mind are very inaccessible, but their impact is always great. India and the Indian mind are very open, but communication is one-way. Nepalis know everything about India, but the Indian people have neither the interest nor the facilities to learn about Nepal. In order to make India listen, Nepalis have started speaking loudly. Only time will prove the worth of bringing up the issue at public debates rather than leaving it for diplomats alone.

The world has been much more relaxed since the end of the cold war. But regional tensions exist which, if not tackled properly, may endanger peace and stability of the region. In spite of the pious wishes expressed on official ceremonies, our neighbours have yet to overcome their hostility toward each other. As a result, there is an artificial sense of restraint even though both are preparing for every kind of confrontation. Relations between nations cannot be taken for granted as is the case with personal friendship. One has to be assured by continuous trials and tests. And Nepal, at present, is undergoing a very difficult trial and test to survive as a nation, that, too, a democratic nation between two divergent but very powerful nations.

(This commentary was first published in Spotlight News Magazine, 26 November 1993)

Index

O

P

Q

R

Third World 3, 6, 129, 168, 190, 197, 200–201, 215

U

V

W

Y

Z